Maximum Tips

Maximum Tips

How to Get the Most Out of Waiting Tables

MenuTree Books

SFO Press
San Francisco

A MenuTree Book
published by

SFO Press
55 New Montgomery Street
San Francisco, CA 94105

FIRST EDITION

Library of Congress Cataloging in Publication Data

Maximum tips.

(MenuTree Books)

1. Waitresses. 2. Waiters. 3. Table Service.
4. Tipping. I. Title.

TX925.M39   1986   647'.95   86-6575

ISBN 0-937741-44-2

---

86 87 88 89 90 10 9 8 7 6 5 4 3 2 1

Thank You...to the waitresses, waiters, and restaurateurs—all top pros—who unselfishly contributed their invaluable secrets of success for this book.

May their tables be always occupied, and their stations always filled, with friendly and *generous* guests.

Contents

1

How to Acquire the Trade Secrets

MOST SERVERS WILL TELL YOU that scoring a job waiting tables is a relatively easy matter. You don't need a business suit for the job interview, you rarely need a resume, and if your timing is right, you don't even need an appointment.

All you need for success in the typical restaurant job interview is an appropriate appearance and a winning attitude—the two traits that are so attractive to restaurant managers who have job openings to fill.

When you look the part and can talk like you know your stuff (or, are willing and anxious to learn), you're most likely to get the job you want. You may even be asked to start the same day.

But in the restaurant business, getting a job is usually the easy part. Learning the techniques it takes to get paid top dollar for your work can be a lot more difficult.

Getting a job at a restaurant where the tips are said to be "good" (averaging 10 to 15 percent) isn't the answer. Good tips, say top servers, are a dime a dozen, they're *minimum* tips. Since so many diners leave a tip for service these days, good tips are almost guaranteed.

"Excellent" tips, however—*maximum* tips that average *15 to 20* percent—are relatively rare.

Yet, in all kinds of eateries—from white tablecloth supper clubs to red checkered tablecloth pizzerias, from revolving skyscraper dining rooms to sidewalk cafes—waitresses and waiters are cruising their stations right now (as you read this) and earning tips that many servers only dream of: tips that average out to *20 percent*, or *better.*

These pros obviously know how to work the room.

How do they do it?

MenuTree Books surveyed top professional waitresses and waiters to discover the techniques they use to succeed with customers, score the best tips, and win the restaurant game.

We also wanted to know how the pros learned their trade secrets.

The School of Hard Knocks

A majority of the servers we interviewed said they learned the rules (and the shortcuts) the long, hard way—through years of experience on the job.

Those who had received any sort of organized on-the-job training usually described it as no more than the most *basic* training.

The typical scenario: Each new server is assigned a few hours of "trailing" another server around the house to learn the layout of the kitchen, dining room, storage room and employee lounge, meet the staff, then receive a typewritten list of house rules, regulations, and procedures.

Trailing may serve as an introduction to the unique requirements of a particular restaurant, but it doesn't provide an insight into the art of successful table service.

Yet for most servers, trailing seems to be the only training available. Opportunities to acquire the *professional techniques* of restaurant table service are scarce. Aside from the formal training traditionally required in America's most elite restaurants, in-depth training in professional table service is usually available only in a select few of the nation's dining establishments.

Recently some of America's corporate-owned and -operated chain restaurants began to offer advanced training programs. But not every server gets—or *wants*—the opportunity of training and working in a chain restaurant. So, advanced training for most servers is still rare.

The harsh reality: *Getting a complete list of the trade secrets of successful table service remains, for most servers, an unlikely prospect.*

Why is there such a shortage of advanced training in the winning moves of table service?

One reason may be that individual restaurant managers don't have the incentive to put servers through a series of productive training sessions. Because of the endless supply of servers (and job seekers who want to be servers), it's often easier and less costly for managers to simply hire and fire until they find enough experienced pros to assemble a top serving team. Waiters and waitresses who flunk the probation period get the pink slip, and the next applicant on the list gets a chance.

Another reason managers are reluctant to teach advanced table service techniques is because restaurant workers who are here today are often gone tomorrow. A job waiting tables is easy to get, and twice as easy to quit. And no manager wants to spend company time and money teaching a treasury of techniques, tactics, and tricks of the trade to a server who may quit a week later to work for the competition across the street.

So, many restaurant managers try to cut their losses by hiring those servers who have already been professionally trained—by the guy across the street.

Most servers, however, have very few opportunities of getting the kind of professional training they need to cut *their* losses, keep their jobs, and score excellent tips.

Now comes this guidebook, and it will help *you* cut *your* losses in the restaurant business with the information you need to succeed.

What's In It For You

This guide will give you the professional methods that are usually available only in the formal, in-depth server training programs you may never have had the chance to participate in. It contains the secrets of successful table service, the tricks of the trade the pros use to earn *maximum* tips with *minimum* hassles.

The book will show you how top servers get things off to a good start with customers by making a positive first impression. How they use, and read, body language. How they recover gracefully from the inevitable mistakes. How they successfully handle complaints. How they turn pesky problems into better tips.

There are guidelines here for building the check by selling more food and beverages. There are suggestions for working as a team player, and for saving time during the rush hours with a variety of shortcuts. There are tips for handling beer, wine, and liquor. And, tips for gracefully handling the problem of customers who drink too much.

Also included are several valuable suggestions for working successfully with managers.

The final chapter, How to Keep Your Share, tells you what you need to know about paying taxes on tips—without overpaying the taxman.

How to Get the Most Out of This Book

To make the most effective use of this guide:

1. Browse through it quickly, cover to cover.

You'll get a general picture of the topics covered, and learn which chapters present the techniques you're most interested in.

2. Read, and then reread, the chapters you find most interesting, and take notes.

Underlining important points (a yellow marker works best) is one good way of learning and remembering information. And writing out the steps to a procedure can be an especially powerful method of memorizing; writing helps you store the information more firmly in your memory.

3. Adopt those table service techniques that are appropriate for your restaurant, and adapt the others to suit.

Serving styles vary somewhat between private supper clubs, for example, and family restaurants. Techniques that are effective in one establishment may be out of place in another.

Customer service is an art, not a science. And these rules are really only guidelines to help *stimulate your thinking*. Obey them, break them, or modify them as you see fit to suit the unique situation, the particular occasion, and the individual customer.

Now, on to the wide-ranging and practical advice from the pros on the techniques of earning maximum tips.

2

How to Get Maximum Tips

LEGEND HAS IT that an 18th century Englishman introduced the custom of tipping to the modern world.

Like a young executive on the fast track, he had no time for long coffee breaks. So upon arriving at his favorite London coffeehouse one foggy day, he dropped a few pence on the table as a friendly bribe for faster service.

He got served immediately—with a smile, no doubt—and his bright idea of offering a tip (to insure promptness) was on its way to becoming a full-fledged custom.

Two hundred years later, tipping survives, but in a slightly altered form. Instead of getting the *tip* first, then providing good service, servers in the 20th century deliver the *service* first, then hope for a good tip.

Somewhere along the way, the tables got turned.

The basic nature of the tip, however, hasn't changed a bit: it's still a strictly *voluntary* contribution.

The dictionary says a tip is a gratuity, a present, a gift given in addition to payment for a service. The Internal Revenue Service sees it a little differently: the IRS considers a tip to be taxable income, not a non-taxable gift.

But the taxman does agree that a tip is a gift in the sense that *the decision of whether to tip, and how much to tip, and who to tip, is left entirely up to the customer.*

Few restaurant goers would argue with the IRS on that point.

But the uncertainty that results from the "service first, tip later" system can be a real problem for servers. Occasionally, after providing ample service, a server gets a scanty tip. Or, no tip at all. It's frustrating, but the brutal truth is, when you're working for tips, you have no guarantee of either fair play or fair pay.

Sometimes you win, sometimes you lose. Each time, though, you work first and find out later how much you get paid (if you get paid). Whether you're serving a single diner, a couple, or a party of ten, one of three possibilities is in store for you at tipping time.

Possibility #1: You get stiffed.

This happens occasionally, for several reasons:

• **When you're serving a large party,** each member
may innocently (or, not so innocently) assume that their host
has either taken care of the tip, or collected enough from
everyone in the party to cover the tip. The host, meanwhile,
expects everyone else to leave their own tip.

It's their mistake, but *you* lose.

• **When you're serving hypersensitive or intolerant people,**
something you say or do may be taken as an insult or a slight,
and used as an excuse to withhold your tip. It's often just a
misunderstanding.

What can you do? Nothing.

• **When you're serving diners who "don't believe
in tipping"** because "it's the boss's responsibility to pay the
help, not the customer's" (and there are uncounted thousands of
these folks out there), again, you're just out of luck.

Getting stiffed after providing good service is rare, but it
happens, and there's absolutely nothing you can do about it.
Nothing *legal*, that is.

Remember: Tipping Is *Permitted*, but never required.

Possibility #2: You get the standard, or normal, tip.

The standard tip is usually between 10 and 15 percent. Fifteen percent is most often mentioned in the *Recommendations for Tipping* section of restaurant guidebooks, but the type of restaurant, the local custom, and the *opinion of each customer* really determines how much is normal or standard.

Possibility #3: You get the maximum tip.

What exactly is a maximum tip? A maximum tip is the best tip each customer would leave under the best of circumstances. It is, for example, the kind of tip restaurant aficionado William Rice calls "a larger tip than normal".

In his restaurant guide, *Where To Eat In America*, Rice offers his readers advice on when to leave the standard tip, when to leave less, and when to leave more:

We generally respond to competent, or even well-intentioned service with a 15% tip, but feel no pangs about reducing the percentage if the job is not done properly.

Surly, inattentive service deserves no reward at all.

If a waiter's performance is outstanding, a larger tip than normal may be in order.

This larger than normal, or *maximum* tip, is the best tip possible from a guest. It's that guest's idea of the standard tip, which you earn just for providing the service, plus an extra bonus which you get for providing special service.

Convincing customers that they've received special service is easy. And as you'll see, it doesn't mean working harder, it simply means working smarter.

According to one waiter's observations, 10 percent of restaurant goers never leave a tip, another 10 percent leave the standard tip no matter what kind of service they receive, and the remaining 80 percent increase the tip for excellent service, or reduce it for less-than-excellent service.

There isn't much you can do about the relatively small number of diners who have that irritating habit of always tipping a flat rate (or a certain percentage), or refusing to tip at all regardless of how outstanding your service.

But there's a lot you can do to encourage generous tipping from the 80 percent majority of your customers who make a mental note of your serving performance and reward you, or penalize you, as they see fit.

Each time you convince them to reward you generously (instead of merely tipping their standard percentage), you score a maximum tip. That increases your average and helps make up for the times you're undertipped or stiffed.

Six Ways to Increase Your Tips

You can convince customers that a larger tip than normal is in order. But since you can't demand, count on, or require a tip, you must *induce* guests to be more generous. Here's advice from the pros on how to do it:

1. Develop rapport with guests.

Connect with customers on a personal level. It's easier for customers to be generous with a warm, friendly, sincere, and personable server who appears to be interested in them.

Cold, remote, and uninterested servers are easy to stiff.

2. Sell more food and beverages.

The more you sell, the bigger the tab. And as a general rule, the bigger the tab, the bigger the tip.

3. Give a little extra—*personalized* service.

The general rule here is, whether people are buying soap, soup, or service, they expect to pay more when they get more. Give them extra service; they'll pay (tip) extra for it.

4. Get assigned to a better shift.

It's no secret that certain times of the day, and certain days of the week, are much better for earning tips than other times and days.

Which shifts are better? According to the conventional wisdom, Saturday night is best of all, Sunday night is the worst, Wednesday night is better than Friday night, nights in general are better than afternoons and much better than mornings.

But this is just the *conventional* wisdom; the best shift for tips in your restaurant may be the Sunday morning brunch.

In any case, here's some good advice for getting assigned the best shifts:

Make the most of your current shift; increase your tips with better sales and consistently excellent service. You'll get noticed. And top servers usually get assigned the best shifts—automatically.

5. Handle complaints effectively.

Mistakes are inevitable. Problems occur no matter how hard you try to eliminate them. More important than eliminating problems is the way you handle the ones that occur. Servers often score better tips because of their ability to gracefully smooth ruffled feathers and fix anything that goes wrong.

6. Develop a following.

You know you're doing the right things when regular customers not only ask for you, but wait for one of *your* tables. They're likely to be your most generous fans.

Repeat business is essential to the success of any restaurant. The more repeat business you can generate for your restaurant (and for yourself) the better your tips over the long run as well as the short run.

What Diners Really Want From You

Restaurant goers in the 80s have several reasons for eating out: to meet friends, to try new foods, to avoid the work of preparing food, or just for entertainment. Whatever their main reason, they all want to feel comfortable wherever they eat. And this, most diners agree, is basically *your* responsibility.

Customers often determine the amount of your tip according to *how comfortable you've made them feel.*

Here are three good ways to make them comfortable:

- **Make them feel welcome.**
- **Make them feel important.**
- **Make them feel that they're getting their money's worth, that you are *earning* your tip.**

Customers need a *reason* to reward you with a larger tip than normal. Convince them that your service is worth tipping extra for. Make them feel they owe you something extra. Persuade them to tip you the maximum by delivering *attentive, careful, and professional service*—maximum service.

Maximum service is outstanding service, but don't confuse it with *constant* service. It's possible to spend very little time serving a customer or larger party, yet leave the impression that everyone received outstanding service and personal attention.

That's because maximum service is based on *quality*, not necessarily quantity. It's the right kind of service to the right guest at the right time.

The only catch here is, since outstanding service often means different things to different diners, various approaches are needed to succeed with each of the wide variety of people you serve. The tricky part is in figuring out early enough which of the extras your guests like and will tip extra for. Different guests prefer different extras.

Learning to read the table makes it easier to determine the kind of service that will be most successful. The next chapter gives you guidelines that will help.

A Word About the Competition

Recent polls show table service to be a major problem area in the restaurant business. One survey found that 75 percent of those questioned felt they were receiving significantly less service than they had in the past. And they were becoming increasingly cynical about the quality of goods and services in general.

In another poll, 80 percent of diners questioned said that even if the food was good, they would not return to a restaurant if the service was poor.

The pros take full advantage of this situation by giving customers what they can't get from the competition. Says one server, "Outstanding service is so rare, customers are usually delighted and often *eager to return the favor* with an outstanding tip! And, why not? Who would you be more generous with—the server who offers you the basic service or the server who does it your way, making all the right moves, usually before you've even had a chance to ask?"

The basic lesson: Give extra to get extra.

4 Ways Servers Lose Tips

1. They neglect to pay attention to details.

Details are important. Some that seem insignificant are the most important to customers. (Cleanliness and hygiene is one area where diners are *very* detail-conscious.)

2. They bungle the job in the final moments.

Last minute errors can be deadly. Your service may be nothing short of magnificent right up to the time when you present the check. Do *that* little job wrong, and you lose points.

Just as film stars are only as good as their last good movie, servers are only as good as their last good move.

The tip isn't yours until it's in your pocket. Don't lose it by making the wrong move at the last moment.

3. They give the impression they're working for tips.

Servers with dollar signs in their eyes lose tips.

Customers would rather get the impression that servers are working not for tips but rather for the sheer joy of satisfying the customer. It may seem far-fetched, but most really successful servers are able to give that impression.

4. They try to predict which of their guests will be the best tippers.

Who are the best (and worst) tippers? Don't waste your time trying to figure it out. Preconceived notions can hurt rather than help you. A rookie server who pays attention to good tipper/bad tipper types gives more attention to a table of two business executives (reputed to be good tippers), less attention to a table of four foreign tourists (reputed to be bad tippers).

The rookie is often in for a surprise.

The pro gives full attention to every customer and lets the tips fall where they may. The pro is often surprised, too.

Pleasantly surprised.

The purpose of this guide is to show you how to get the maximum tip from every one of your guests, not just from diners who are considered to be good tippers. The more you help guests think to themselves, "That was dynamite service!" or "She is one outstanding waitress!" or "That waiter really knows his job!", the more you'll find on your tip tray.

Use Every Trick In the Book

On the following pages, you'll find suggestions from the pros about 1) what to do and what to say, 2) what *not* to do and what *not* to say, and 3) how to set up a successful serving routine.

Your objective is simple: To serve each customer the way that customer likes to be served. The tips in the following chapters will help you accomplish that objective.

3

How to Get the Winning Image

THE SUCCESS YOU ACHIEVE in earning maximum tips depends entirely on you.

Average tips are yours for minimum effort, but the best money in this business comes to you as a reward for the extra effort that you make *at the right time* and *in the right way.*

More than just extra effort, it's extra effort that's performed intelligently. You get maximum tips by working *smart*, not by working hard. To work smart, you need to have your act together if you want to perform successfully in your professional role as *attentive host.*

Getting your act together—developing your abilities as a professional server for top performance at every table—requires your attention in these three areas:

- **Your appearance** (the first thing customers notice)

- **Your attitude** (the second thing they notice)

- **Your approach** (the way you handle your job)

This chapter deals first with the way many successful servers view their jobs—their *attitudes* toward waiting tables. It then presents some guidelines for adapting a winning image—the *appearance* that attracts better tips. The remaining nine chapters of the book present the pros' suggested approach for developing a professional serving routine.

The Right Attitude

Successful table service begins with the right attitude. But first, a few words about the *wrong* attitude.

When we asked servers, What's the worst attitude to have about this job?, the overwhelming majority gave this answer: *Believing you're in a subservient and humble job.*

No pro considers herself or himself to be working in a subservient role. Subservient means useful or helpful, or of service, but in an *inferior* or *subordinate* capacity.

This attitude is self-defeating. Servers who feel inferior, act inferior. And by their obsequious and fawning behavior, they actually invite customers to kick them around. Perhaps they confuse the word "serve" with *servile*, a word that describes cringing, overly submissive behavior.

Acting deferential or diffident with customers hinders your ability to succeed even more than acting *superior* does.

An inferiority complex, as well as a superiority complex, can only hurt in this business.

Feeling *equal*, however, will do you a world of good.

Another way servers limit their success is by refusing to *play the role* of a pleasant, eager, attentive host. They contend it's dishonest to try to be someone you're not, to "put on a phony personality just to earn money."

But the pros say playing the role doesn't have to be phony or dishonest. You can be yourself and play a role at the same time if the role you play features your best qualities and downplays your worst.

Don't get hung up on the idea that playing the role means suppressing *the real you*. In the brief time you have to relate with your customers, they'll never get to know the real you, anyway. Give them the *professional* you.

The professional you is 1) Enthusiastic, 2) Self-confident, 3) Flexible, 4) Amiable, and 5) Resilient. You've probably already got these qualities in your own "real" personality. All you have to do is use them to best advantage in your role as attentive host.

5 Qualities of an Attentive Host

Successful attitudes differ according to individual personalities. But a good attitude (a successful one) should include five important qualities:

1. Enthusiasm—*An intense or eager interest.*

Your enthusiasm doesn't have to be (and shouldn't be) the bubbling-over kind. Just a show of interest—in your work, in your menu, in your restaurant, and in your customer's comfort.

Give guests a message that you really care about them, if you want them to care about you.

2. Self-confidence—*The belief in one's own abilities.*

Be self-confident. It puts people at ease to feel that when they're seated in *your* station, they've got a server who knows the restaurant business (*and*, has good connections in the kitchen.)

When you appear confident about your job, your guests will be more able to relax, content in the feeling that they are in good hands.

Caution: *Don't let self-confidence run wild.* A cool and detached, superior manner doesn't work any better than a fawning manner. Few people are more obnoxious than the proverbial *surly* waiter. (The days of earning big tips by intimidating wimpy diners are over; most restaurant goers have finally caught on to the scheme.)

Your best approach: Quietly, but confidently, convey your talent to perform like a pro.

3. Flexibility—*The ability to change or modify direction.*

Do a quick study of each customer and adapt your behavior style to mesh with theirs. This doesn't mean changing or distorting your personality in any way. It simply means modifying your serving approach to help your customers get comfortable.

Example: A laid back and mellow manner that works so well with, say, a group of tourists with 3 hours for lunch will be less appreciated by a party of business executives who are frantically trying to cut deals with each other (and eat at the same time) during a 45-minute lunch break.

A winning idea: Adapt your approach to be like your guests. Stay mellow with mellow customers; give fast-track business executives snappy, efficient attention.

The most celebrated salespeople are experts at adapting. A top salesperson who normally talks fast adapts quickly with a slow talking prospect. Within seconds, voila! A slow talking salesperson. And then, bingo! Another sale.

It's self-defeating to stick to formalities when guests obviously prefer to be informal. It's equally impractical to be informal when formality is more appropriate.

4. Resilience—*The power to recover strength and spirits quickly.*

All the good advice in the world can't guarantee problem-free customer relations in the restaurant business (or any other service business). Some restaurant goers are mean and nasty by nature and once in awhile, you'll find them seated in *your* station responding to your courtesy with their own brand of rudeness.

How can you defend yourself against this frustrating behavior?

Develop the ability to bounce back immediately from insults, indignities and brickbats. *Consider the source,* and accept these irritations as one of the hazards of the job.

The danger in letting it get to you is that it can affect your performance (and your tips) at other tables. Don't let a chain reaction get started. One jerk can ruin your whole day, *but only if you let him (or her).*

Responding to rudeness with politeness is a difficult assignment, but this tip will help: *Get your ego out of the way.* Successful waiters and waitresses are not quick to take offense. They attribute annoying acts and insulting words of customers to ignorance (the boors don't know any better), and they simply refuse to take insults or criticisms personally.

The pros are specialists in getting along with other people.

5. Amiability—*The quality of friendliness that makes one likeable.*

It's easier to like someone who likes you. Let your customers know that you like them, and get them to like you in return. You'll virtually eliminate the hassles of waiting tables; customers are less likely to hassle a server they like.

And it almost goes without saying, diners are likely to be more generous with servers they like.

Getting to like your customers isn't the impossible mission it might appear to be. There's something to like in everyone, even some of your most obnoxious regulars. (If their good qualities aren't obvious, keep looking.)

Letting customers know you like them isn't difficult either. One way to do it: Show your cheerful desire to be helpful. Another effective tactic: Show your sense of humor. Nothing relieves the tension of a new relationship faster than a laugh.

And if you can make some self-effacing comment along the way that shows you don't take yourself *too seriously*, you'll have people on your side in no time flat.

How to Attract Tips With Your Appearance

Looks aren't everything, but in the restaurant business an attractive appearance does attract tips.

Don't be concerned if you don't have the physical attributes of a fashion model. A winning appearance for the restaurant game doesn't require perfectly chiseled features or an hourglass figure. It simply requires what anyone can achieve: impeccable grooming and appropriate style.

Because you're in the business of serving food, the *squeaky-clean* look is highly recommended. Anything less than perfect grooming tends to distract diners in a negative way.

Some immediate turnoffs: dirty hair, dirty hands and fingernails, soiled uniform, body odor, bad breath. And there are no exceptions to this essential rule: *Never go to work needing a shower.*

Neatness is important too. Diners who are served by an unkempt server wonder what the kitchen looks like. Is the cook a slob too? Appetites disappear. Sometimes, the customers themselves disappear.

If you don't see many sloppy, unkempt servers, it's because they don't last long in this job.

7 Appearance Checkpoints

Here are some guidelines that are crucial to achieving the kind of successful image that distinguishes top servers from the rookies. Follow these steps to a winning appearance that attracts tips, not negative attention.

Here's what the pros suggest:

1. Keep your hair short.

Or, tie it up or back. Or, if local laws require, tuck it under a hair net. A healthy head of hair looks great on you—but one stray strand on a plate or in a bowl of soup is guaranteed to put the damper on a diner's carefree mood.

2. Use cosmetics with moderation.

Makeup and lipstick? Sure, but keep it light, and appropriate for your complexion.

3. Avoid fragrances.

Perfumes or colognes? It's much better to skip them. But if you insist, keep your scent subtle so you don't overpower the aroma of a charcoal-broiled steak.

4. Wash your hands often.

Clean hands are an absolute must. Your hands are always on display. Diners hate to see dirty hands serving food that they're counting on to be clean and healthful.

It's also a good idea to use a hand lotion if you have dry skin.

Another important point: Keep your hands off your hair and face when you're with customers.

5. Shape your nails.

Short- to medium-length is best. They're easier to keep from breaking, and they're easier to keep clean.

As for nail polish, a neutral (light red, pink, or clear) shade of polish draws less attention to your hands. No nail polish may be best of all.

6. Avoid wearing excess jewelry.

Travel light. Leave the heavy stuff at home. Anything more than a ring and a watch, a simple gold or silver necklace, and small loop or stud earrings on this job is superfluous.

Noisy bracelets, long necklaces, or flashy rings can get in your way at the worst of times.

7. Keep your uniform (or costume) clean.

Most food stains can be removed by plain soda water or lukewarm tap water and mild soap. But get to it before the stain sets. Find out early about spot removers and special cleaning instructions for the fabric.

Have a spare costume at work for emergencies. You should own at least two spares: one at work, one in the laundry.

And here's a tax tip: You can deduct on your income tax form the cost of your uniforms, and the cost of having them cleaned.

Your Own Personal Dress Code

If your restaurant neither supplies uniforms, nor requires you to furnish your own, it's up to you to choose the uniform that gives you the right image. Here are some guidelines to follow if you wear street clothes to work:

1. Choose your image to fit your restaurant's style.

A conservative look is probably best; you'll hardly go wrong in any restaurant wearing the standard white shirt (or blouse) with dark slacks (or skirt). A sport shirt and jeans, though, might be more appropriate in a beer-and-burgers cafe, while Hawaiian shirts and shorts are hot at any eatery on or near the beach.

The most effective strategy: choose the look that's appropriate for the house and the customers.

2. Choose darker colors that hide stains.

Wine, oil, vinegar, and other stain-makers will be better absorbed by dark colors, especially black. (Some patterns of Hawaiian shirts hide stains very well, too.)

3. Wear neutral hose.

Your best bet: natural or coffee color, no visible reinforced areas, and no runs. Keep at least one extra pair at work.

4. Wear comfortable shoes.

Your best bet in shoes: a style with closed toes and low (or flat) heels in a color that matches your costume, if possible. Rubber (or crepe) soles give you better traction; you're less likely to slip on a wet floor.

More on Creating a Positive Image

Walk tall. An important part of your overall appearance (and success) is your *posture*.

What has posture got to do with tips? Plenty. Good posture (chin up, back straight, stand erect on both feet) indicates a professional bearing. You *look* as if you know what's going on.
(Even when you don't.)

Two ways to improve your posture: 1) Tone up muscles with regular exercise; 2) Consciously think about standing straight. It also helps to wear comfortable shoes.

The Ideal Image

The clean, natural, conservative look works best in the restaurant game because it's a *safe* image that neither draws attention nor offends.

The pros always look their best because, whether it's fair or not, diners judge servers first by their appearance. And that first impression is the lasting impression.

Adopt the appearance of a pro. It's just one more way of increasing your chances of attracting the maximum tip.

Some Tools of the Trade

Besides a uniform of some sort, and an order pad (provided by your restaurant), you'll also need:

1. A pen.

Actually, you'll need several pens because pens get lost in restaurants more often than socks in Laundromats.

Bic ballpoints are popular for a couple of reasons. First, they're inexpensive. Second, they have a sort of anti-theft feature: they're not retractable. So whenever you loan your Bic to someone, *hold on to the cap*. Pen borrowers are a lot less likely to put an uncapped pen in their pocket than a retractable ballpoint.

2. A lighter.

You may not smoke. You may even dislike those who do. But servers who light customers' cigarettes are popular with smokers; everyone else seems to be against their smoking.

Carry a small disposable lighter with you. But hang on to it; light cigarettes with it but don't loan it out. Lighters disappear faster than pens.

3. A watch.

Any cheap, old watch that keeps time will do. In fact, an old watch is better than a new watch, and a cheap watch is much better than an expensive watch. Leave the expensive jewelry at home; you don't want to look like you don't *need* tips.

4. A corkpuller.

Corkscrews may become the buggy whips of the restaurant business. Get a cork puller with two prongs that slide down either side of the cork. It makes cork-pulling easy.

On Your Way to Work, Remember...

1. Never start a shift in a bad mood.

It's absolutely amazing how many stupid, ignorant, rude, impudent, penny-pinching non-tippers you meet when you're in a bad mood!

2. Smiling is okay.

The most powerful expression available is the old standby: the sincere smile. It's an expression that works wonders everywhere on earth.

The sincere smile has helped sell used cars, launch love affairs, win political office, soothe hurt feelings, spread warmth and good cheer.

It also helps servers win maximum tips.

Customers love it when you smile. They often ask servers who aren't smiling, to smile. They never ask smiling servers to stop smiling.

3. Everything tastes better when somebody nice serves it to you.

The most exquisitely-prepared delicacies are marred by mediocre service.

But a great server can improve even the most mediocre meal.

4

How to
Make the Team

WHO MAKES BETTER TIPS, servers who work tables by
themselves, servers who work in teams of two or three assigned
to a table, or servers who, along with the entire staff, provide
service whenever and wherever it's needed?

The pros have various reasons for preferring one of these
popular systems over the others but we found no consensus among
the experts on which system is best for tips. Each has its
advantages and disadvantages:

1. Individual table assignments.
Each server is assigned a certain number of tables for which
she is totally responsible.

She pockets all tips earned from those tables and splits a
portion (usually 10 percent) with a buser.

Advantages: Servers who work tables individually have a
better chance of developing a personal rapport with customers
which usually leads to better tips.

Disadvantages: When the rush is on, it's sink or swim. A
server who begins to sink with no one around to help, sinks (and
suffers the consequences) all by herself.

2. Two- and three-server team assignments.

One member of the team works the table, taking the food and drink orders and serving the drinks; the other members work the kitchen, placing the order and serving the food.

Two- and three-person teams split all tips evenly before splitting again with busers.

Advantages: Help is always available during the busy times. Some servers claim this system is better for tips since customers believe they are getting twice as much service from two (or more) servers. Others strongly disagree.

Disadvantages: If one of the team members leaves a negative impression with guests, the others may suffer a reduced tip. Personal rapport between diner and server is less promising.

3. The "everyone serves" system.

Servers are assigned tables for ordertaking only. Table service is carried out by the entire serving staff. When a food order is ready, the first server available delivers the order. By the end of the meal, a party may have been served by several different servers.

In this system, tips are pooled and at the end of the shift, totaled and divided among all servers.

Advantages: Service is quicker since food orders never sit in the kitchen waiting for the assigned server.

Disadvantages: Same as the previous system: tips are not as good because service is not as *personally* attentive. Since customers don't connect with any one server, they are less apt to feel extra generous as they might with a server they had a chance to get to know.

Which system works best for servers? The most likely answer: Professional servers can make any system work in their favor when they make it their goal to serve each customer the way that customer likes to be served.

But whether or not serving teams are set up in the dining room, the pros agree that servers are more successful when they're working as part of the Big Team with support from the entire staff—in the kitchen, the dining room, and even the business office. Teamwork in the restaurant business, they insist, is a prerequisite for success.

Teamwork Eases Tensions

A restaurant crew that works as a team and supports each other (even when assigned individual tables) earns better tips and attracts more loyal customers than a crew of servers working competitively.

Servers who compete with each other for good tables, for favors from the kitchen, and for tips, create an uncomfortable tension in the air that can be felt by everyone in the dining room. When guests feel that tension, it interferes with their ability to relax.

Teamwork prevents that kind of tension and helps create a comfortable atmosphere. And, as everyone knows, relaxed, comfortable diners are easier to serve, and tend to be more generous.

The Right Staff

Here's how a good team works together:

1. Nobody says, "That's not my job."

Each member of the staff is interested in making each customer as happy as possible. Requests from any customer are taken by any server and (if tables are assigned) quickly relayed to the server in charge of that party.

Requests for water or napkins, or to replace dropped silverware should *not* be relayed but should be taken care of immediately.

No server returns to the kitchen empty-handed; when dishes should be removed from a table, the server who notices the need first does the busing. And everyone stays on the lookout for tables that need clearing.

2. Everyone helps others when they need it.

That way, *everyone* gets help when they need it.

Note: Each server takes responsibility for his own station first. Assisting other servers is necessary for a smooth running dining room, especially during the rush hours, but help should never be offered at the expense of one's own customers. No one should neglect his own guests to help out at another server's table.

3. Everyone keeps everyone else informed.

How much time is it taking the kitchen to prepare a certain dish? How quickly is the Daily Special moving? Is a shortage problem developing somewhere?

Everyone stays in touch to avoid surprises.

How to Get Along With (Almost) Everybody

Everyone in the restaurant business operates under pressure.

You get pressure from your manager and your customers. Your manager gets pressure from customers, the owner, the bank, the city health officials, the competition, the restaurant critics, and the staff.

The rest of the staff (chef, kitchen assistants, hosts, busers, and dishwashers) get pressure from you, the customers, and management. (The kitchen crew works, not only under pressure, but in intense heat as well.)

The restaurant business is not a good place for people with short tempers.

One way to ease the pressure and keep tempers from flaring is by using *politics* wisely.

You can't escape restaurant politics anymore than you can escape office politics; it comes with the territory. But you can learn to make politics work for the benefit of, rather than to detriment of, team spirit.

Politicians have given politics a bad name. The word *politic* describes someone who has practical wisdom, someone who is prudent, diplomatic. And wisdom, prudence, and diplomacy can make working together a pleasure.

Here are some of the ways you can make politics work to everyone's benefit.

1. Take the initiative in meeting people.

When you start a new job, begin immediately to build friendships. Don't wait for people to come to you; take the first step yourself.

2. Be tactful with co-workers.

If someone is interfering with your job by not doing theirs right, try a little diplomacy. Instead of getting mad— "Don't ever take a request from one of my customers without telling me!", try *You can help me if you just tell my customers you'll send me over to take their request.*

3. Never correct anyone in public.

They don't like it (or deserve it) any more than you do.

4. Be on time to work.

The dining room can be a hectic place even when everyone is pulling their share of the load. One server arriving late makes it tougher for the others who have to cover the extra station.

5. Treat your buser with care.

And, with a generous split of the tips. Busers always seem to work harder for servers who do that.

6. Don't ignore common courtesy.

If you want to get along well with others, common courtesy will help you do it. Courteous people show consideration toward others. They're polite and well-mannered. They're eager to do favors for others. But they're in short supply.

Being courteous will lift you above the crowd.

How to Manage Your Manager

It's a cinch that if you don't get along with your manager, your job (if you're able to hold on to it) will be less than a joy. Here are some tips from managers on what it takes to make them happy:

1. Get organized.

Know your job and your house procedures. Be on time to work, and on top of your work when you're on duty.

This will make you more efficient, and efficiency is one of the traits managers like.

2. Get enthused.

When you see something that needs doing (or are asked to perform a certain job), do it, do it right, and do it without having to be asked twice.

Show an interest in the job and an interest in learning more about the job.

3. *Stay* enthused.

Some servers start a job full of vim and vigor, but soon begin to lose interest. When you let boredom affect your performance, both your manager and your customer will notice.

Neither will be favorably impressed.

4. Forgo excuses.

Don't use an excuse to answer a complaint or a request.

When your manager approaches you about a problem, it's best to handle it quickly and quietly. Whether it's your fault or not, get the discussion over with as soon as possible. Here's how:

• **Acknowledge the problem.**
Yes, you're right, that shouldn't have happened.

• **If it was your fault, apologize.**
Sorry, that was my fault. If it wasn't your fault, don't blame others; skip immediately to the next step.

• **Express your interest in preventing the problem from reoccurring.**
Your fault: *I won't let that happen again.* Not your fault: *How can we avoid that in the future?*

A straightforward, businesslike approach (with good eye contact) works wonders with managers who are trying to solve problems. Excuses are the last thing they want; they want results.

Do they need to learn who was at fault? Not from you (unless it was your fault). If you're wrongly blamed, it won't hurt just to silently let it ride. Chances are your boss will discover soon enough that he wrongly blamed you. Then, you gain in two ways: you earn respect for not getting upset over trivial details, and your manager realizes *he owes you one.*

A Dozen More Reasons Why Managers Like Top Servers

Top servers are tops with managers because they have a positive attitude, an ability to communicate, an attractive appearance, a warm smile, a sense of humor, a good disposition, and a professional bearing. They also have intelligence, sensitivity, good manners, confidence in themselves, and they know their jobs well.

5 Reasons to Be Tolerant When Managers Err

Managers slip up from time to time. Some will even admit it. But whether they admit it or not, a savvy server tolerates most managerial snafus because she or he understands the problems most managers face in their jobs:

- *They earn less per hour than many servers*

- *They're required to work more hours*

- *They have more problems to deal with*

- *They have more crucial decisions to make*

- *They work under more pressure*

And that goes double for managers who also own the place.

How to Manage the Chef

Top servers agree, chefs are pretty wonderful people, but they can get a little testy in the extreme heat of the kitchen. And testy chefs can make things exceedingly difficult for servers who annoy them, or complicate their work.

If the chef is not on your side during your shift, you may be fighting a losing battle.

Here are a few tips for getting the chef on your side:

1. Make friends with the chef.

Give the chef some attention. Show a sincere interest in the food and the chef's methods of preparing it. The chef is a culinary artist (or, would like to be) and is likely to respond well to a little recognition of his or her expertise.

2. Print your orders clearly.

Anything you can do to eliminate confusion and mistakes is worth doing.

3. Follow all kitchen procedures exactly.

Show an interest in making the chef's job easier. Is there anything you can do to make things work more smoothly?

4. Pick up finished orders quickly.

No chef likes to see food, cooked to perfection just moments ago, sit undelivered and unappreciated under a heat lamp.

Get the hot food out hot, and the cold food out cold.

But don't stand around waiting for an order; it puts a subtle pressure on the kitchen. Keep busy in the immediate area, and stay alert to the kitchen output.

5. Send compliments to the chef.

Deliver credit where credit is due. Don't fail to bring a customer's "Bravo!" back to the chef.

(If customers never ask you to bring compliments to the chef, it may be because they are too shy. So it is perfectly acceptable to bring compliments of your own invention to the chef from time to time, especially when you think the chef could use some good cheer.)

6. Never criticize the chef.

No good whatsoever can come from this.

Whenever you bring a dish back to the kitchen, phrase your request in the chef's, not the customer's, favor.

Don't say: *You cooked this steak rare; the guy wants it medium.* Better: *Could we put this back on the grill for a few more moments? The guy changed his order from rare to medium.*

How to Be More Efficient

You can work hard, and accomplish a great deal. Or, you can work efficiently, and accomplish even more—with less effort.

Efficiency makes your work so much easier and quicker, it's worthwhile to find more efficient ways of getting everything done, especially the sidework.

Efficient work is less exhausting: the energy you save is physical, mental, and emotional. You'll reduce your chances of accidents, and save food and materials.

Here's what the experts suggest:

1. Look for shortcuts.

Think of each chore you do and try to come up with a quicker and better way to do it.

(But don't sacrifice quality for efficiency.)

2. Decide what needs to be changed.

Are you wasting time? Or energy. Or both?

3. Analyze the job.

Get the whole picture. Consider each job as three steps:

1) Preparation
2) Doing the job
3) Cleaning up

Then ask yourself a few questions: Why does this job take so much time? Why is it so difficult?

4. Work out a better method.

Or eliminate the job entirely if it's not completely necessary.

5. Use two hands whenever possible.
This will cut your work almost in half.

6. Conserve your energy.
Keep your hand and body movements short and simple.

7. Get comfortable.
Stand straight. Sit straight. Put your materials and tools in a logical order, and nearby to minimize reaching.

8. Make each trip count.
Never walk anywhere empty-handed.

9. Carry an extra pen as a back-up.

10. Use a tray to carry more—*both* ways.

How to Go Off Duty

Here's the smooth way to finish your shift and go off duty when some of your guests are still at your tables:

1. Introduce your guests to the server who will cover your section.
I am going to be leaving now. This is Linda, and she will be happy to get you anything else you may need. Thank you!

2. Give Linda an envelope with your name on it for the tips your remaining guests will be leaving for you.

5

How to
Master the Menu

RESTAURANT GOERS OFTEN ASK a myriad of questions
about menu choices before making a decision:

Is the fish fresh?
Are potatoes included?
Does your chef use MSG?
Is that cooked in real butter or margarine?
Do you have any decaffeinated tea?
Can I have carrot cake instead of the carrots?

Diners have always been interested in quality, portion size,
and substitution possibilities. Now, they're becoming curious
about cooking styles, methods and ingredients.

One of the reasons for this new interest is the modern
diner's search for a healthier diet. Another is the concern over
scientific data that links various food additives to common
allergies.

There's also the possibility your guests are "foodies"—
restaurant groupies who keep in touch with the latest recipes
and hot new cooking styles that often accompany the opening of
hot new restaurants.

But whatever the reason, you can be hit (when you least expect it) by a barrage of questions on any aspect of your product—from the size of the appetizers to the origin of the zucchini.

You've got to be prepared. Here's why:

1. You'll save yourself valuable time.

Whenever you have to stop for even a moment to search your memory or your menu for the answer to a customer's question, or go to the chef, the manager, or another server for the answer, you lose precious minutes.

Under the pressure of a rush-hour crowd, just a few wasted minutes can throw you hopelessly behind schedule. That makes it tougher to earn good tips.

2. You'll reduce the chances of diner dissatisfaction.

Customers quiz you about the food because they want to know what to expect. Diners hate surprises from the kitchen. A customer who gets an unwelcome surprise from the kitchen is a dissatisfied customer.

The better you are at preventing surprises, the less chance there will be of problems.

3. You'll reinforce your image as a pro.

The simple fact is, people do expect you to *know everything* about your job.

Demonstrating to them that you're a real pro who is always on top of things increases their confidence in you and reduces their anxieties.

4. You'll increase your ability to sell.

One of the surest ways of increasing tips is by selling more and building the check. And a successful selling strategy, presented in Chapter 7, is built on this basic requirement:

Know your product.

Get on intimate terms with your menu, and your success in food sales will improve dramatically.

What Not To Do If You Don't Have The Answers

Don't rely on an alibi, or try to get off the hook with a standard excuse. Excuses identify you as a rookie. Even worse, weak excuses invite sarcasm from smart-alec guests. An excuse rarely works for you, and usually against you.

So, what to do if you don't have all the answers? *Get* the answers. Your only successful strategy with customers is to be prepared.

All You Need to Know About Your Menu

Mastering your menu is not as difficult a chore as you might imagine. All it takes is knowing which details are important, then following a few short steps to quickly memorize them.

First, a look at the details your customers are most interested in and likely to ask you about. Then, some shortcuts for storing it all in your memory.

Here's what you need to know.

1. The item inventory.

Become familiar with every item that's available from the kitchen: its name (and correct pronunciation); its location on the menu; whether its an appetizer, an entree, a side order, a dessert.

Also: Which items are included with which entrees? Which orders include salad.

Know the customary accompaniments to entrees, side dishes, desserts, and drinks. Some typical examples of accompaniments: Tartar sauce and lemon wedge with fish. Onions, ketchup, mustard, mayonnaise, tomatoes, and pickles with hamburgers. Lemon and sugar with tea. Cream with coffee. Syrup with pancakes.

2. The item substitution policy.

Depending on house policy, this can range from "No Substitutions" to "anything goes."

3. The quality of each item.

Is the fish fresh or frozen? Is the beef choice, prime, or good? Is the fruit fresh or canned? Is the lobster from Maine or Mexico? Is the soup homemade or canned?

4. The preparation method for each item.

Is the chicken boiled or broiled? (Over charcoal or mesquite?) Baked or braised? Basted or fried? (Pan or deep? In butter or oil?) Grilled, microwaved, panbroiled, poached, roasted, sauteed, steamed, simmered, or stewed?

5. The ingredients of each item.

Have accurate answers to questions such as, Is that prepared with salt? MSG (Monosodium glutamate)? Butter?

Winging it can be risky; your knowledge of ingredients is important to diners on salt-free, sugar-free, or fat-free diets, and even more important to those with allergies.

Learn the ingredients of the house dressing.

6. The time required to prepare each item.

How long does it take to cook each dish? Which items have been prepared in advance and can be quickly reheated? Which are made-to-order?

Which are cooked in the oven? In the microwave?

Which are precooked, then heated to serving temperature when ordered? Which are prepared and kept at serving temperature on a steam table, in a refrigerator, or on ice?

Preparation time includes the time to cook the item and get it on the plate. It varies according to several changing factors: the current workload in the kitchen, the ability and efficiency of the chef and kitchen crew, the availability and efficiency of the kitchen equipment.

As a general rule, experience is the best teacher when it comes to knowing preparation times. But watch out for changing conditions that can throw your good timing out of whack.

7. The price of each item.

For obvious reasons, you need to know all menu prices.

That's it. Now, here's an easy way to learn it all.

3 Short Steps to Menu Mastery

Getting a firm grasp on all the menu facts you need should be easier for you if you follow these steps:

1. Do your homework.

Get a copy of the menu and take it home.

Choose one part of the menu—the appetizer section, for example. Study it closely, reading it aloud. Then write it out from memory. Repeat the process until you have it completely memorized. Move on to another section.

This basic exercise—saying everything out loud, then writing it down—helps to plant the facts deep in your memory. At this stage, you're filing away the general information you need to write an order accurately.

The next step is to dig for the details, the supporting background information that gives you the answers to specific questions. For that research, it's best to go directly to the top boss in the kitchen.

2. Interview the chef.

Ask questions and take notes on preparation methods, preparation times, ingredients, substitutions, quality, and any other aspect of the dish that a customer is likely to ask about.

Get the correct pronunciation of any foreign words on the menu.

3. Immerse yourself in the facts.

Rehearse in your mind the answers to diners' questions. Talk about food with friends, co-workers, and customers. A few days of studying even the longest menu should be enough time to make you an expert with an answer to every menu question.

That's the kind of serving performance that pays off.

3 Ways to Give Yourself the Edge

The best-paid servers are those who go the extra mile. Try these powerful tactics to get way ahead of the crowd:

1. Discover the chef's specialty.

Not the Chef's Special, but the chef's specialty, the one item the chef likes best, and prepares best. When a guest asks you for your special suggestion, you can't go wrong recommending the chef's favorite dish.

2. Perform your own taste test.

Make an effort to sample everything on the menu.

Some savvy managers hold staff dinners to give servers a chance to sample the food and wine. If your manager isn't doing this, suggest it.

If staff dinners are out of the question, ask the chef to help you study the product. As you sample, take notes of your impressions.

Another good idea: Get the chef's description of the appearance, aroma, consistency, and taste of each dish. Add these impressions to your own.

3. Prepare a list of original descriptions.

It's tempting to take the easy way out and resort to tired, trite, and overworked words and phrases to describe your products. Resist the temptation. Look for words that really describe the food. But don't discard commonly used words if they provide accurate descriptions. If a steak is tender, it's tender.

Be poetic but don't overdo it. Avoid cliches that invite yawns, snickers, or groans: Special, Classic, Delicate, Famous, Secret, Delicious, Original, Exclusive, Exotic, Cooked Our Way; Cooked To Perfection.

How to Cope With Change

The product that's available from your kitchen can change from month to month, day to day, or hour to hour. Be aware of new items and changes before starting your shift; then keep on top of changing conditions.

Keep close tabs on:

• The daily specials.
The soup of the day, the chef's special, the available pies and pastries.

• The daily shortages.
If the kitchen is running short on some items, you'll want to know about it before you take an order for that item.

It's disappointing for diners to count on fresh lobster only to learn the bad news five minutes later: "I'm sorry, but it seems we're fresh out of fresh lobster."

It's not much fun, either, for servers who have to deliver that kind of news.

6

How to Break the Ice

AS CUSTOMERS WALK INTO a restaurant, they immediately begin looking for some sign of welcome.

Waiting even half a minute for attention puts many people in an anxious mood. They begin to wonder, Does anyone know we're here? Does anyone care? Did we come to the right place? Are we going to get decent service?

A pro, even when busy with other tables, *never* walks by a table of new guests without offering a greeting of some sort. It's good insurance against customer hassles. *Hi! I'll be with you in a moment,* even when spoken on the run with a tray full of hot food, gets things off to a good start:

1. It lets people relax.

Immediate recognition tells customers they're okay. It identifies you as their server, and prevents them from worrying about being ignored or forgotten.

Try to connect with new guests within sixty seconds of their arrival.

2. It takes the pressure off.

Customers can be impatient when they're waiting for service, even when the place is jammed and it's obvious that everyone's working at a feverish pace just to keep up.

Assuring new customers that you'll be with them "…in a moment" buys you time. Guests who know they're next on your list, are likely to give you all the extra time you need to catch up.

3. It marks you as an attentive pro.

People are especially impressed to see that you've considered them important enough for an immediate welcome, even though you have four other tables full of demanding diners frantically waving at you for attention.

That's a powerful first impression to make on customers.

The First Word in Successful Table Service

The best way to greet new customers is with a simple *Hello!* Or use one of the standard variations whenever it's appropriate: *Hi!*, *Good morning! (afternoon!) (evening!)*, *Howdy!*, *Waddaya say?*, *How ya doin'?*

The point is, use some form of *hello* first.

"Welcome to Blank's, are you ready to order?" has an impersonal, recorded-message ring to it, the kind of opening line some managers insist servers use to ensure uniformity. It never works as well as a warm Hello.

"How many in your party?" is too abrupt to serve as a courteous greeting.

A courteous greeting often gets dropped in the rush to get people seated and served. But that's a poor strategy. Don't take the greeting for granted; your guests certainly don't! Say hello to as many members of the party as possible; it takes only a few extra seconds, and it's worth every second.

After you say hello, then what? What's the best way to relate with each of the various personalities you're about to serve?

To determine how best to relate to individual customers, the pros use a few techniques for reading people. (Actually, since time is short, they *speed* read people.)

They're looking for the answers to these three questions:

- Why are these people here?

- What sort of people are they?

- What do they expect from me?

The better you're able to answer these questions about your guests, the better your chances of serving each one the way that customer wants to be served. In this chapter are some techniques for reading people you can use to get the answers quickly.

Close Encounters of All Kinds

Reading people quickly and accurately can be tricky. It helps to start with a few generalizations about restaurant goers.

Why are these people here?

Restaurant goers have various reasons for eating out.

Why did your guests come into your restaurant and take a seat at your table? Here are six possibilities:

1. **They're looking for social contact.**

2. **They're celebrating a special occasion.**

3. **They're talking business away from the office.**

4. **They're avoiding the cooking and the cleaning.**

5. **They're "foodies" in search of the perfect meal.**

6. **They're just hungry.**

You'll probably want to use one approach with business executives, for example, and a different approach with families celebrating anniversaries. Relating to foodies who are intensely interested in the details behind the dish will no doubt be different than relating to diners who are interested only in getting something to eat.

What sort of people are they?

Professional servers suggest that you can divide your customers into two main personality types:

1. Assertive
2. Responsive

Assertive diners like to be in charge, they like to take command. They speak up, and talk fast. They make decisions quickly, and they make eye contact regularly.

Responsive diners act the opposite: they respond to your taking charge, they speak softer and slower, take more time to make decisions, and make eye contact less often.

The pros adapt their serving approach to complement their guests' personalities. They are assertive with responsive types, responsive with assertive guests.

The reverse strategy doesn't work as well. Assertiveness in servers is often seen by assertive guests as *challenging* behavior. They want you to *respond* to their wishes, not challenge them.

And responsive behavior in servers is often regarded by *responsive* guests as nonchalance, or even apathy. *Asserting* yourself with responsive people tells them you're in charge, in control, and ready to take responsibility for seeing to it that their dining experience is a success.

What do they want from me?

Restaurant goers have various preferences about styles of table service.

But you can safely expect their preferences to fit into one of three categories:

1. Formal and unobtrusive

2. Informal and friendly

3. Friendly welcome followed by serious service

A typical example of category 3: *I like servers to begin with a friendly and open approach, then get the order to the kitchen, and back to the table promptly, see that everything is taken care of with very little fanfare so that I hardly know they are here. The right stuff appears at the table at the right time, and disappears the same way.*

Which approach is most likely to succeed? Base your decision on clues you get from your guests.

Helpful as they are, these are all generalizations. To really zero in on your guests' motivations, personalities, expectations, and definitions of *excellent, outstanding, personalized* service (the kind that attracts the maximum tip), you need some techniques for reading people.

How to Speed Read People

Discovering the best way to relate to each of your guests *as an individual*—is probably the trickiest part of your job. One problem is the shortage of time; you rarely get more than a few moments to size up customers and determine the best approach to take.

Another problem is the complexity of the human personality.

Nevertheless, to succeed in the restaurant business, you do need some way of understanding and effectively dealing with a wide variety of people.

Top servers size up people quickly by collecting clues from their appearance, their speech, their body language, and the situation at hand. Your customers' age, clothing, facial expressions, and companions, all provide clues that will help you reduce the complexity of customer relations.

Fine-tune your first impressions. Watch for specific signals (read their body language), and listen for subtle verbal messages. The pros follow these steps.

1. Take note of the situation.

Customers behave one way when they're having an ordinary dinner together, another when they're celebrating a special occasion in a large party. They are also likely to change their behavior slightly during business lunches, then again during after work get-togethers with friends.

Their basic personalities aren't changing but their moods are. And that affects the way they relate with their companions, and with you. Use your awareness of the general situation to tailor your approach to your guests.

2. Listen intently.

Careful listening is crucial to learning about people. It's especially important when guests are ordering. Questions and comments may contain subtle information about your guests' personalities in addition to the obvious ordering instructions.

3. Observe body language carefully.

Body language is a means of communicating without words. We send messages, consciously or unconsciously, with a meaningful glance, expression, gesture, movement, or mannerism. Even the way we stand or sit sends a message to others about ourselves.

Body language can be complicated and confusing. Reading it accurately depends on many variables. But just being aware of it increases your ability to read it and cut through the fog when someone's verbal communication contradicts their non-verbal message.

Body language can give you a general idea about people. Are they open and friendly? Aggressive? Timid? Nervous? Look for both conscious and unconscious messages. Facial expressions, gestures, and mannerisms all convey messages.

Body language, like a foreign language, becomes easier to read when you read it regularly.

A Few More Generalizations

Whether your guests are assertive or responsive, formal or friendly, craving good food or craving good times, it's a good bet they all want you to make them feel a) welcome, b) important, and c) respected.

They like to feel they're getting personalized attention. Here are some suggested strategies for giving the right amount of personal attention to diners in three different, and typical, situations:

1. Single diners.
Strategy: Pamper them. Eating out alone is difficult for many people; regardless of their age or background, they often feel intimidated, unwelcome, or uncomfortable.

Move their order fast, ahead of others when possible. (You'll retrieve the table faster for larger parties.)

2. Couples.

Strategy: Give less attention to amorous couples, more attention to couples who aren't getting along. (Time moves slowly for people who are not talking; get 'em fed and move 'em out.)

Married couples often like prompt service but may prefer more leisurely service if they're celebrating a birthday or anniversary.

Younger couples may welcome an informal relationship with you; older couples often prefer quiet, dignified service.

3. Groups.

Strategy: Older men? Be firm and friendly. Older women? Friendly and efficient. Boisterous men (or women)? Self-assertive and friendly. Businessmen or businesswomen? Quiet and efficient. Mixed groups? Unobtrusive and efficient. Family groups? Friendly and efficient.

Be Ready to Adapt

Sometimes, the approach you thought would work isn't working.

Be sensitive to your customers' mood and their reaction to your behavior. If they aren't responding in kind to your friendliness, perhaps they want a more formal style of service.

Change your game plan.

Guidelines For Good Conversation

Good conversation, like body language, is an art, with its own set of rules. Here are some of the most important ones:

1. Approach customers facing them.
Don't try to talk with people over their shoulder.

2. Look them in the nose.
The *bridge* of the nose, actually, right between the eyes. Eye contact is less intense that way, less apt to intimidate a shy guest, yet it indicates that you're giving that person your full attention.

Whenever you have something to say to a large group, move your attention around from person to person. Try to make brief eye contact with everyone. Whenever you're speaking to customers, look at *them*, not the wall, not out the window, not at people walking past the table.

3. Smile.
A sincere smile says a lot.

It says you love your work. It says you welcome and enjoy your guests. It says you understand their needs. It says you are a professional and attentive host.

4. Be a good listener.
It will help you know what to say and what not to say.

13 Unspeakable Acts

What to say usually comes naturally.

Some things that should never be said may also come naturally.

Here's a list of topics, remarks, manners, and subjects to avoid with guests:

1. Don't talk about last night.
Don't mention a guest's previous visit unless your guest brings it up.

2. Don't talk about company matters.
Don't discuss the job, the boss, the money, the chef (except in glowing terms, of course.)

For most people, gossip about another's job is either completely boring or only mildly interesting and can do you more harm than good.

3. Don't talk about other customers.
Obviously, your guests will wonder what you tell other customers about *them*.

4. Don't discuss politics, religion, or racial subjects.
These topics are just too hot for most people to handle in a place where they came to relax and have a good time.

5. Don't discuss sex.
Avoid conversation that might be considered risque. You risk offending *someone*—if not at the immediate table, then perhaps at a nearby table.

6. Don't get personal.

Never ask people what they do for a living, or where they live, or how many times they've been married and divorced, unless they make it obvious that they want to talk about it.

7. Don't get smart.

Avoid being flippant, wise, sarcastic, cheeky, or brash, even in fun. With friends, this kind of humor is (usually) acceptable. With people who don't know you very well, it can be deadly.

8. Don't get bossy.

Avoid the appearance of giving orders to customers.

9. Don't complain, gripe, rant or rave.

No matter what's bothering you, it's unprofessional behavior.

10. Don't argue.

Don't try to clear up trivial misunderstandings.

11. Don't embarrass guests by correcting them.

12. Don't talk down to elderly or handicapped guests.

You'll get much better response from everybody (kids included) if you relate to all guests as mature and capable adults.

13. Don't talk about yourself.

And don't worry about finding something clever to say. Courtesy and good manners are much more important than clever conversation. Good manners will help you relate successfully with anyone (and everyone).

Good food is essential to restaurant success. But, since good food is available in most restaurants, it takes good customer relations to make a successful restaurant a *roaring* success.

Your relationship with diners must necessarily be short and somewhat superficial. Get things started off on the right foot; otherwise, you may never have a chance to recover. The way you start is the way your customers expect you to finish.

Break the ice with a warm welcome, observe your guests closely to discover their preferences, and project the image of a careful, attentive professional.

The generous rewards make the extra effort worthwhile.

7

How to Build the Check

TOP SERVERS KNOW how to sell. And it pays off.

The pros use a technique called *suggestion selling* to increase their tips by increasing their check totals. Always on the lookout for opportunities to sell more food and drink, they earn a lot more than servers who are content merely to take orders and deliver food.

Since the tip is usually figured as a percentage of the tab, it follows that bigger orders lead to bigger tips. Here's a typical example of how a little selling effort can build the check, and the tip:

A party places an order for four dinners that include soup or salad, and coffee. The tab comes to $46.90 before tax. The group tips 15%—the server pockets $7. A good tip.

In another station, another foursome places a similar order. But this server takes the order, then suggests an appetizer before dinner. The group decides to share two appetizer orders. Then, while pouring coffee after the meal, the server mentions a few dessert possibilities. This time, four desserts are ordered. The tab, which started at $46.40, now totals $64.40 before tax. These four diners, stuffed but happy, also tip 15%—$9.60. (Actually, they round it off and leave a ten dollar bill.) A maximum tip.

The first server works hard and earns a fair tip. The second server works *smart,* and collects an extra three dollars for very little extra effort.

And that's at *only one table.* A few extra sales like that at, say 10 tables, can mean an extra $30 or more over the course of a shift. Multiply that bonus by five shifts for an easy $150 per week raise.

Of course, the opportunity to sell isn't present in every serving situation. When it is there, it pays to take advantage. But when the opportunity to sell is obviously missing, it's better to forget about selling and simply get the order.

When to Sell, and When *Not* to Sell

There are two basic rules to remember before trying to sell:

1. Know when *not* to sell.

Not all of your customers will be receptive to suggestion selling. Some diners know exactly what they want to order and are resistant to any kind of assistance. They may actually *resent* a suggestion, even when you offer it in a helpful way. Watch for clues that say, "I know what I want, just take my order and don't try to sell me anything."

Example: You exchange a few opening pleasantries with the couple at your table. Then, the host immediately begins to rattle off the order: "I'll have the top sirloin, rare, baked potato, oil and vinegar. She'll have the same, medium, but with mashed potatoes, and bleu cheese dressing. And water. Thanks."

You may be tempted to ask, Would you like to order wine? An appetizer? The daily special? A side order of something? Coffee?

Don't ask! This is obviously a diner who wants to be in charge. He's probably considered, and dismissed, all other menu possibilities (for himself as well as for his companion). Your suggestions are most likely to be rejected. The "Thanks" at the end is the giveaway; it means, "That's all. Got it?"

(You still have a chance, however, to sell desserts and coffee. Wait until the end of the meal and see how things are going.)

2. When in doubt, sell.

While some customers will give you very clear signals about whether they're receptive to your suggestions, others are harder to read. When you get no clear indication that selling would be unwelcome, try it. You can always back off if you get the *don't-try-to-sell-me* look.

Studies show that servers who promote food, wine, and desserts, maximize their returns. You can't build a bigger check if you don't try.

What Exactly is Suggestion Selling?

Suggestion selling in a restaurant, like all successful selling, is a sincere effort to *solve customer problems.* And your guests do have a problem: Getting what they want from the kitchen. They may not even know what they want. It's a great opportunity for you to *help people buy,* help them choose from the menu the best combination of items.

Building the check by suggestion selling is easy—for two reasons. First, your customers are already pre-sold. And second, your strategy is simple: *assist and suggest*.

Restaurant goers come in to eat, not to browse. They're going to buy *something;* the question is, What? Which of your products do they want? How much of your product do they want? You may be able to influence your guests' buying decisions in a way that benefits you as well as them.

Restaurant customers like suggestion selling for several reasons:

- It helps them make a decision from a menu that has too many choices. Your recommendation is welcome.

- It helps them make a decision between two choices that look especially appealing; your suggestion about one or the other dish may help.

- It helps them, if they dine out infrequently, or are too timid to explore something new, to order things they're only slightly familiar with. Suggesting wine, for example, often prompts a smile: "Oh, yes, wine, of course! What kind do you have?"

Suggestion selling is easy because it's low-key. This is *not* a hard sell method. Rather, it's the softest of the soft sell. It's as simple as offering the right suggestions to the right customer at the right time.

Suggestion selling doesn't require a sales pitch because it's really less a matter of selling than it is consulting.

Suggestion selling is simply one more element of *attentive* service.

NOTE: Don't confuse *suggesting* with *advising*.

Diners want suggestions, not advice. Giving suggestions that sound like advice can be risky. Advice is often construed as an indication that the guest has made (or is about to make) a mistake. Avoid using phrases such as "You should order this," or, "If I were you, I would order that."

Unlike advice, suggestions are *neutral*. A suggestion is simply a statement of what is available. It leaves the impression that, whatever the guest decides, that's the right decision.

Customers respond positively to suggestions from servers with whom they have confidence and trust. When your words and your manner send out the message, *I'm here to help you,* you'll win their acceptance and confidence.

What You Need to Know for Successful Suggesting

A little preparation goes a long way toward making suggestion selling successful:

1. Know your product.
You need to know what you have available to sell. You need to know how to put combinations of menu items together to make a sale. A feeling for popular combinations of entrees and side dishes, or various alternatives that may click with difficult-to-please guests, gives you the edge.

Anticipate obvious requests. If you're listening carefully to guest's questions and comments, and you know which side dishes are complimentary, you'll be able to suggest the naturals—items your guests want, but may not have thought of.

2. Know your customer.

The more you know (or can gather) about your customers, the better chance you'll have for making intelligent suggestions that they'll accept. Of course, you don't have much to go on other than your first impressions of guests, but just a few moments of observation may be all you need.

Here are a few general suggestions for acting on your general impressions. Are your guests:

- Obviously high rollers? *Suggest the pricier entrees.*
- On a budget? *Suggest the lower-cost specials.*
- On a diet? *Suggest the low-calorie specials.*
- Tourists? *Suggest the local specialty.*
- Celebrating? *Suggest champagne, fancy foods, desserts.*

Any large party is likely to say "Yes!" to everything you offer—from cocktails to desserts—when they're celebrating a special occasion such as a birthday, anniversary, or winning the lottery, enjoying a night on the town with friends, or are trying to impress a business client.

12 Easy Steps to the Sale

1. Size up your guests.
Adapt your presentation style to your customers.

2. Use a positive and creative opening.
Open every sales opportunity on a positive note.

Don't ask, "Are you ready to order?" Your customers hear this worn-out phrase every time they dine out. Try something different to set yourself apart from the crowd.

Use a creative opening instead of a boring one:

What can I bring you for breakfast?
Have you found something you like?
What would you like for dinner this evening?

3. Start selling right away.

The best time to suggest a before-dinner drink is before the food order is taken.

The best time to suggest specials that are not on the menu is before your guests have had a chance to study the menu.

The best time to start selling is the first chance you get.

4. Sell from the best angle.

Lean slightly toward your guests as you write. This subtle mannerism shows that you're attentive and interested in accurately getting their order.

Whenever possible, move around the table to each guest for the order.

5. Look for expressions and gestures.

To sell, you must communicate with your customer with eye contact and body language.

Watch your customers' body language for signs that they are receptive. You know when you're on the wrong track when they fold their arms, frown, constantly look away, close their fists.

You'll know that you're on the right track when you see a relaxed customer with open palms, eye contact and smile.

The body language that says *open and interested* is as easy to see as that which says *closed and turned off*. All you have to do is be aware this language exists, and watch closely for it.

Look for "Help!" signs. Watch for opportunities to offer suggestions. If a guest stares blankly at the menu, hesitates while ordering, or flashes you a puzzled look, try one of these polite questions:

May I answer any questions about the menu?
May I offer any assistance with the menu?

6. Listen carefully.

Ask questions and actively listen to the answers. Very often, your guest will be telling you what he wants *in general.* Then it's easy for you to suggest an appropriate specific item from the menu.

7. Ask questions that narrow the choices.

Do you like very spicy food, or not so hot?
Do you prefer chicken, or beef?

8. Be responsive.

Nod. Smile. Use appropriate facial expressions. Throw in a few "Uh-huhs" now and then. Show you are interested.

Look at your guests while they're answering your questions, even if they're not looking at you. It helps you to concentrate on really hearing the answer, and it also let's you see if an expression or gesture might change the meaning of the answer.

When you're doing the talking, look at your guest. When you make a suggestion while looking somewhere else, it communicates disinterest. And it invites distrust.

Note: One time you may want to look away is whenever your customer is giving you a "No" answer. You're suggesting; they're shaking their head. Drop the eye contact and look away for a moment at your order pad, or the menu, or something on the table. It's a subtle way of neutralizing the negative feeling from the refused suggestion.

9. Be enthusiastic.

Accentuate the positive. Say *Yes* as often as possible. Try to avoid using the word "No" whenever you can make an answer sound like "Yes."

Example: Your customer has just asked you to bring mushrooms with his steak instead of salad. Don't say, "Sorry, sir, that's not one of the permitted substitutions." Too negative. Instead, try: *Yes, sir, I can bring you a side order of mushrooms.*

Important: Emphasize the words *side order* so that you don't give the impression that the extras you suggest are included in the price of the meal.

10. Use the best price strategy.

As a general rule, suggest items in the middle- to high-middle price range. Suggest the most expensive items only when guests are clearly high-rollers.

11. Be specific.

Don't say: "Would you like an appetizer?" Better: *Would you like to start with a plate of fresh clams?*

Suggest any dish your chef or restaurant is noted for, anything particularly unusual, or delicious, or famous, or prized.

Respond specifically to requests; it's your best chance to sell. When a guest asks for your recommendation, "What would you suggest?", or "What's good today?", don't say "I don't know, I haven't eaten here today", or "Everything's good", or "Marsha, this guy want's to know what's good. What's good?" Some better responses:

- *The Special is getting lots of compliments.*
- *The veal is excellent.*
- *We're famous for our Eggs Benedict.*
- *Two items are especially good today…*

12. Use descriptive phrases.

Fresh fruit. *Hot, spicy* apple pie. Describe your suggestions in an appetizing way. Avoid mundane descriptions, or repeating menu descriptions.

But be realistic. Don't call a hamburger a *fine-ground super-colossal jumbo-juicy melt-in-your-mouth heavenly burger.*

(Unless that's exactly what it is.)

Specific Selling Strategies

Here are some selling strategies that work:

1. Cocktails.

Advice on how to suggest a cocktail varies. Some pros say, forget it, a cocktail drinker doesn't need a hint; if they drink, they'll order one before you've had a chance to ask.

Others insist that the familiar "Would you like to order a cocktail?" or "Would you like something from the bar?" is perfectly acceptable and likely to offend only the strictest teetotalers. Size up each situation; use your better judgement.

2. Appetizers.

A good opener: *Would you like me to bring your salads right away or would you rather begin with a shrimp cocktail appetizer?*

If the food order requires a long preparation time, tell your guests; then, suggest an appetizer for the meantime.

Show them you're on *their* side: If your appetizers are served in generous portions and your guests are hesitating about having an appetizer, suggest they order just one and split it: *One order is often enough for two people...if you would like to split one, I'll be happy to bring you each a separate plate.*

Better to sell one than none.

3. Side dishes.

When they order an entree without the obvious and usual accompanying side dish (a burger or steak without fries or onion rings), suggest the obvious side dish. You can always phrase it as a clarifying question: *Oh, and did you want fries with your steak?*

4. Desserts.

After clearing, *prepare your party* for dessert. Crumb the table. Replace napkins. Empty ashtrays. Refill water glasses. Then, suggest a *specific* dessert: *Are you ready for coffee and perhaps some fresh blueberry pie ala mode?*

If you can think of a better way to sell desserts, try it.

3 Things That Make Selling Easier

1. Rapport.

Make a connection; establish a bond of trust and confidence. People are more likely to trust someone they like and more likely to accept suggestions from someone they trust.

2. Enthusiasm.

Your guests will be more convinced of the merit of your suggestions if you are *enthusiastic* about them. It sends the message that you are making suggestions that you think will be appreciated.

3. The Bandwagon Effect.

You'll find it's much easier to suggest and sell to others after selling to one member of a party.

What to Do When Your Suggestions Aren't Accepted

Don't fret—your guests are not rejecting you, they're simply rejecting the suggestion. Don't let "No, thanks" stop you from looking for other selling opportunities.

The pros never miss a selling opportunity.

8

How to Handle Drinks & Drinkers

TWO OF THE NICER THINGS about wine:

1. It enhances the pleasure of dining out, and
2. It helps build the check—*and* your tip.

The more you know about wine, the easier it is to *sell*. And the more you know about beer and liquor, the easier it is to *serve*. (Liquor and beer don't need much of a sales effort—most drinkers already know what they like.)

But many diners panic when it comes to ordering wine; they're just not sure which wine to order. This is where you come in.

We asked the experts to put the subjects of wine, champagne, liquor, and beer into perspective.

First, some advice for selling wine:

• At your first encounter with each party, mention the wine list. *Good evening. Have you seen our wine list? We have some recent additions that may interest you.*

• If your guests have expressed an interest in ordering wine, you might successfully drop a suggestion after they've decided on the entree: *Since you're all having fish, we have a very good Chardonnay that would be an excellent choice.*

A Short Course in Wine

Which is the best wine to recommend to guests?

Which wine is best depends on a number of things including the mood, the food, the setting, the time of day, and, of course, the drinker's preference.

But there are some traditional guidelines you might follow when guests ask for your suggestions:

1. Lower priced wines are usually a good bet for occasional wine drinkers.

These wines are often chosen by restaurant wine buyers because they are suitable for the majority of customers who are neither wine experts nor aficionados.

2. It's hard to go wrong suggesting a young, white wine.

Not only is the age of white wine less important than the age of a red, but a dry white wine generally goes with any food better than red. It's especially good with seafood.

A sweet white wine is a good suggestion when guests order fruit or desserts.

3. It's also hard to go wrong suggesting Beaujolais.

This light all-purpose red wine also goes well with virtually all food.

But the age of a Beaujolais is important. Check the vintage date; it should be less than a year old.

4. When guests ask for a wine to go with a specific food, suggest the traditional combinations.

For example:

- Beef: *A full-bodied red such as Bordeaux*
- Poultry or pork: *A light red or white*
- Lamb: *A light red or pink*
- Glazed ham: *A sweet Sauterne or Zinfandel*
- Veal: *Chianti or Barbera*

The idea is to choose wine and food that will compliment each other, and avoid a combination where the wine overpowers the food (a hearty red wine with fish) or vice versa (charcoal broiled sirloin with a light white wine).

Don't be intimidated by the art of wine selection. Even the experts (*especially* the experts) disagree on many points.

5. Table wines are often a good suggestion.

These house wines are also chosen by wine buyers to be acceptable to most restaurant goers. They are usually an inexpensive red, white, or rosé wine, poured from a gallon jug or dispensed from a wine keg.

The normal six-ounce serving fills a standard 8-ounce wineglass 3/4 full. These wines are often ordered by the carafe, either a half-liter or a liter. White and rosé are served chilled, red is served at room temperature.

How to make house wine special: Find out the name, year, and character of the house wines. Describing them in these terms , rather than simply "the house red" (or white or rosé) improves the image of any wine.

6. Suggest a dessert wine instead of dessert.

Dessert wines are usually served either of two ways, straight up in a 3-ounce sherry glass or on the rocks (over ice) in an old fashioned glass.

Some popular dessert wines:

- *Port, either ruby port (dark red) or tawny port (amber)*
- *Sherry*
- *Dubonnet*
- *Vermouth, either dry (pale color) or sweet (darker).* As after dinner drinks, these are not exactly at the peak of their popularity but you may occasionally get a request for one or the other on the rocks with a twist.

Keep in touch with latest wine fashions. Popular drinks come and go (then sometimes come back again). Recent favorites are the wine spritzer (white wine with club soda) and the wine cooler (red wine with lemon mix).

How to stay ahead of the game: Watch for upcoming drink fads in magazine advertising.

How many servings are in a bottle?

A full bottle (750 ml. or 25.4 fluid ounces) serves six guests one glass each. Or two guests three glasses each. (Each glass is an 8 ounce wine glass half-filled.)

Is the wine ritual all that important?

Yes, to wine drinkers who have ordered an old (and expensive) red wine.

The ritual was designed to make sure the guest receives the exact wine and year as ordered, and that the wine has not gone bad (turned into vinegar) while in storage.

Modern winemaking methods have virtually eliminated the chances of getting vinegar in a wine bottle. But the ritual lives on.

Here's how it goes:

1. Present the unopened bottle (label up) to the person who ordered it.

Repeat the order aloud: *Sonoma Vineyards 1984 Zinfandel, sir.*

2. Open the bottle.

a) Cut away the foil at the top

b) Wipe around cork with a clean white napkin

c) Insert corkscrew down the center of the cork (stop before piercing the inside end)

d) Lever the cork up about an inch, then pull it out.

If you're using a double-prong cork remover instead of a corkscrew, insert the prongs down the sides of the cork, pushing first on one prong, then the other; turn the handle as you pull out the cork.

3. Offer cork to host.

The purpose of examining the cork has been to determine before tasting whether the wine has gone bad. But many wine experts now feel that cork-sniffing is obsolete and merely an affectation.

For the record, though, here's the customer's traditional cork checking procedure:

a) sniff the cork for the scent of vinegar
b) squeeze or roll the cork between thumb and forefinger and look for moistness and firmness.

Expect a few wags to respond to this step with humor:

"You're serving Cork Au Vin tonight?"
"This cork is obviously rare; I ordered it medium."

But if your guest is seriously participating, wait for approval of the wine before pouring. If your guest is simply ignoring the cork, go on to the next step without comment.

4. Pour an ounce into the host's glass.
Grip the bottle with your right hand, your left hand under the neck of the bottle.

A serious wine drinker will quickly, quietly, and without fanfare *look* at the wine, *sniff* it, *swirl* it in the glass, *sniff* it again, *sample* it, then give you a nod of approval to pour for other guests.

5. Serve other guests.
Fill their glasses to half-full, then fill host's glass to half. Set the bottle near the host with the label facing the host.

Don't be surprised if serious wine lovers ask you to soak the label off the wine bottle for them. Take the bottle to the kitchen, put it in a bucket of warm water, give it a few minutes to soak off, place it between two napkins or paper towels to dry, then present it with the check.

A Short Course in Champagne

How should champagne be served?

With *finesse!* Champagne (or any sparkling wine) is under high pressure in the bottle.

Things should go smoothly, however, if you follow these steps:

1. Bring champagne to the table pre-chilled in an ice bucket which has been half-filled with ice and water.

Place the ice bucket on the right-hand side of the host, either on the table or on a floorstand near the host's chair. Sparkling wines, rosé wines, and white wines may also be served in an ice bucket.

2. Show the label and say the name.

3. Remove the foil from the bottle.

Loosen and remove the wire hood.

4. Remove the cork—slowly.

With a clean white napkin, grip the cork, and turn the bottle. The cork should pop out with force from the pressure.

Another recommended method to allow the gas to escape: rock the cork out slowly.

Caution: Hold the bottle upright, not at an angle, and not aimed in anyone's direction.

5. Pour a full glass for each guest.

6. Return the bottle to the ice bucket or to the table if no bucket is being used.

A Short Course in Beer

What is there to know about beer?

Plenty, if you want to serve it right:

1. Memorize the beer list.

What to do when you don't have the customer's brand:
Don't suggest a *specific* substitution; to many beer drinkers, there is *no substitute* for their favorite beer.

Instead, try: *I'm sorry, we don't carry* Bullfrog Draft. *May I offer you something else?*

2. Check that beer glass.

Is it dirty? Send it back to the dishwasher. Is it hot (just came from the dishwasher)? Cool it down quickly with cracked ice, or get another glass.

It's poor form to present a warm glass with a cold beer.

3. Pour beer correctly.

In some establishments, the servers pour the customer's first beer. If this is the policy in your house, pour it right: Down the middle to the bottom to start the head, then quickly tilt the glass and pour down the side. Try to bring a 1 inch thick head right up to the top.

4. Don't be too quick to pick up an empty.

Remove a beer drinker's empty bottle only when he: a) orders another, b) moves it out near the edge of the table (which usually means "Take this bottle, please" or "I'll have another, please"), or c) leaves.

Beer drinkers don't mind having a few empties around when they're having more than one. (It helps track of how many more than one they're having.)

A Short Course in Liquor

1. Get to know your bartender.

Bartenders can help take the work out of learning about drinks. They can help cut through the confusion you may have trying to become familiar with over a hundred different drinks by name, the type of glass, the garnish, and your part in building the drink.

Also, get to know your bartender's method. They often have a formula they use, a pattern they follow, to get a lot of drinks made correctly when the pressure is on. They may want you to order drinks in a certain sequence, set up glassware in a particular order, call for drinks using a common code.

The methods they use to make their job easier may seem at times to make yours tougher. But top servers say, do it the bartender's way; it's easier in the long run.

2. Memorize the common drinks and brands first.

Ask your bartender for the top ten most popular drinks, and the most popular name brands. There's no reason to memorize drinks and brands you never get a call for.

3. Read a bartender's manual.

You won't need to *study* it unless you want to tend bar. But skimming through a good manual will give you a helpful acquaintance with a wide variety of drinks and drinking lore.

4. Remember customer's drinks.

When it's time for a re-order, the rookies have to ask, "Now, tell me again, what are you drinking?" The pros *remember*, and it's as impressive as remembering customers' names.

Make a mental note of who's drinking what when you take the order the first time. If you get stuck, and your guests are running a tab, look at the tab. Or look at their empty glasses for a memory refresher.

If you're *really* stuck, phrase your what-are-you-drinking questions as verifying statements: *"Vodka-rocks-twist, and a screwdriver."*

If you're wrong, they'll tell you.

5. Code identical-looking drinks.

You take an order for an Irish Coffee, a Mexican Coffee, and a Kioki Coffee. To avoid making your customers do a sniff-and-sip test when they get their drinks, code those drinks at the bar.

The easiest method is probably with stirrers. The Irish gets one stirrer, the Mexican two, and the Kioki, three. Remove the extra stirrers as you serve the drinks.

6. Announce the drink as you serve it.

It's a nice touch that confirms the order.

7. Do the housekeeping.

Replace wet cocktail napkins. Remove discarded stirrers. Keep ashtrays empty.

Drinking, the Law, and You

What about the legal responsibilities of serving alcohol?

Changing attitudes in the 80s about fitness and health, and drinking and driving are causing sweeping changes in the restaurant business.

A recent poll showed that 66 percent of Americans said they drink alcohol, but 29 percent reported that they had cut back and were drinking less than they had the previous five years. The trend appears to have led to reduced sales of alcoholic beverages in restaurants.

But while adults are drinking less, teenagers are drinking more. And 22 percent of the poll's respondents under the drinking age said they have no problem getting served a drink in a restaurant.

This trend, combined with valiant efforts by various groups to get drunk drivers off the highways, has led to recent changes in the way the law regards those who *serve* alcohol.

New laws that increase *servers'* liability are being written, and laws that have been on the books for years are being cited in courts in an effort to place responsibility on servers and bartenders for injuries caused by drunk drivers.

So, waiters and waitresses who serve alcoholic drinks *may be held liable* for the illegal acts of their guests.

Restaurant owners have reacted in several ways. Some have posted signs saying that intoxicated people won't be served liquor.

Others have begun "designated-driver" programs: One person in a party of two or more is asked to refrain from drinking alcohol and take responsibility for driving the others in the party home. The non-drinking driver is given a free dinner and non-alcoholic beverages.

But even without an in-house program, you can do two things to help reduce drinking-related problems for yourself and for your guests.

First, eliminate the incidence of underage drinking: earnestly check identification cards.

Second, reduce the occurrence of overdrinking: diplomatically refuse to serve guests who are drinking too much.

How To Check An I.D.

Checking a customer's identification is often a cause of anxiety for servers. Don't feel nervous about asking; guests who appear to be near the legal age get carded regularly. If they're old enough to drink, they'll have an I.D.

The only guests who are likely to show offense are those who are underage and are trying desperately to convince you they're of legal age. Don't fall for it. Serving a minor can cause *big headaches:* your restaurant may lose its liquor license, and you and the bartender may be arrested.

You may be personally liable for serving an alcoholic beverage to anyone under your state's legal age.

Checking an I.D. is easy when you do it this way:

1. Be firm but pleasant.
May I see your I.D. or proof of age, please?

2. Accept only I.D.'s issued by a federal, state, or local government agency.

For example, a state drivers license, non-driver state I.D. card, military I.D., or passport are usually safe to accept.

Not acceptable: birth certificates, temporary drivers licenses, college I.D. cards, or employment I.D. cards.

3. Check the expiration date.
Is it current and valid? If not, the card is worthless.

4. Check the date of birth.
Know the current cutoff date.

5. Check the picture and description.
When in doubt about an identification, check with your manager.

Be courteous when checking I.D.'s, but don't be shy.

And, don't forget to say thank you.

Cutting Them Off

You've served them, and now it suddenly becomes obvious that you've served them *too much*. Legally, you're required to cut them off. How do you give a drinking guest the bad news?

This can be tricky business, but you can handle it if you keep these points in mind:

1. Use tact when refusing to serve someone another drink.

Don't say: "I think you've had enough." Instead, try: *I'm sorry, I can't serve you another. It's the law.*

Soothe a drunk's ego; don't bruise it.

If the imbiber is friendly, try a little humor to lighten up the occasion.

If, on the other hand, the souse is rude, call management immediately to handle the chore.

2. Try to keep inebriated guests around for awhile until they sober up a bit.

Sometimes free coffee helps keep them from leaving; it won't sober them up, though—only time will do that. But whatever you can do to stall a drunk from driving is worth doing.

It's almost impossible to prevent drinkers from drinking too much. The best you can hope for in one of these uncomfortable situations is that you will have already established a good rapport with intoxicated guests when they were sober.

It's just possible they'll remember you as okay, and accept your cutting them off—without protest.

9

How To Prevent Complaints

YOU CAN'T PLEASE all of the people all of the time.

With the techniques in this chapter, though, you can please *most* of the people *most* of the time. And that will significantly reduce the number of complaints you have to deal with.

Complaints about service fall into three categories:

1. *Inattentive* service
2. *Careless* service
3. *Unprofessional* service

The most effective strategy you can use to avert customer complaints in these areas is, Plan Ahead: *Prevent problems before they occur.* That's your best hedge against hassles.

In this chapter, details on how the pros do it.

How to Prevent Complaints of *Inattentive* Service

You can't give everyone 100 percent attention. But you *can* give everyone the *impression* you're giving them complete attention.

Try these effective methods:

1. Anticipate requests for condiments and non-food items.

Example: You've just taken an order for burgers and fries. Before you bring the order to the table, bring the salt, pepper, ketchup, mustard, horseradish, steak sauce, and mayonnaise.

Whatever customers are likely to want or need should be on the table even *before* they realize they want or need it. Are the burgers big and juicy? Bring plenty of napkins right at the beginning. And when you see they're getting used up fast, bring more without being asked.

Think ahead. It saves time and aggravation.

2. Anticipate requests to clear the table.

Don't let dirty dishes pile up. Clear immediately anything no longer needed by the customer. Plates which have been moved to the edge of the table, or off to one side, are ready for the dishwasher.

Whenever you're unsure whether your guest has finished, ask. Politely.

Not: "Are you finished?" or "Can I take that?"
Better: *Shall I take your plate?* or *Would you like me to take your plate?*

3. Fix small problems before they become big problems.

When guests drop silverware, deliver replacements immediately; don't make them wait.

Note: Whenever you're replacing a dropped fork, spoon, or knife, bring the clean one first, then pick up the dirty one.

Sometimes you'll get requests from customers in another server's station. When they request a no-cost item (silverware, napkins, condiments), bring it yourself. But if the request is for an addition to the food order, your best reply is: *Yes, ma'am, I'll send your server right over.* That eliminates the chance of confusion when, moments later, customers repeat the order to their own server "just to make sure."

Beware: "Sorry, this isn't my table" is almost guaranteed to generate complaints.

4. Always check back.

This is controversial: Some experts say servers should never interrupt diners to ask if everything is satisfactory. Yet others strongly advise returning to the table after three minutes or so to make sure there are no problems.

In any case, all agree that it pays to stay on the alert for needs, requests, or signs or trouble at every table in your station. Customers who have to keep looking for you when they need service can't concentrate on their dinners or their companions; they begin to get agitated.

Give every table a quick glance each time you're in your section. Watch for eye contact and body language that signals a request for attention.

Don't ask, "How is *everything?*" or "Is *everything* all right?" Be specific. Try, *How is your breakfast? (lunch?, dinner?, fish?, steak?)*

Keeping your eye on the table is especially important when you're not busy. Restaurant goers can forgive a little inattentive service when they see you're busy, but when they know you *aren't* busy, they have much less patience.

5. Replace ashtrays often.

It's easier if you replace them before they overflow.

To keep ashes from flying around, use the *cap method:* Place a clean ashtray upside down over the dirty one, pick them up together, then set a clean one down in the same spot.

Give *each* smoker an ashtray. Never replace two dirty ashtrays with only one clean one. Whenever you replace one dirty ashtray on a table, replace all dirty ashtrays.

If an ashtray has a burning cigarette in it, ask the smoker to retrieve it. An announcement like, *Here's a clean ashtray for you* usually does the trick.

Dump ashtrays in a safe container. Make sure not to mix the ashes with anything burnable such as napkins or table cloths. Restaurant fires have been started from one small (but very hot) ash dumped in the table linen bag.

When the house burns down, you're out of work.

6. Keep coffee cups filled.

Tunnel Vision

Some servers, when busy, travel between table and kitchen looking straight ahead to avoid getting stopped along the way.

If they don't make eye contact with a customer who wants attention, they assume customers will just shrug and think to themselves, "Well, I guess she just hasn't seen me yet."

Customers are rarely fooled by this ploy. They can sense when servers ignore their attempt to get attention. Their need may be simple *(More butter, when you get the chance?)*, or an emergency *(Do you have a sponge? This soda I just spilled is soaking into the chair.)*

Pretending not to notice is not the best way of convincing customers to give you a generous tip.

A better strategy is to acknowledge their signal with a smile and a nod. The unspoken message, *I'll be with you in a minute,* wins points. It lets guests *relax*—while waiting their turn.

(If the signal you get is frantic, get right over to the table and investigate; it could be a minor emergency.)

How to Prevent Complaints of *Careless* Service

Before your party takes a seat in your section, you should have removed all the potential sources of trouble.

1. Give your guests a clean table.

Prevent the possibility of anyone sitting at a dirty table.

Carry two towels—one to clean the table top and one to wipe it dry. Replace dirty linen.

Make sure the chair or seat is clean.

Check the condiment containers for drips.

2. Give them a *complete* setup.

If your tables are set before customers arrive, check to see that each setting is complete. It'll cut down on the number of fix-it requests.

Are any condiment bottles, napkin containers, or sugar bowls empty? Fill them or replace them. Burned out candles? Replace them.

Remember that place settings at one table may get borrowed by someone at another table. So don't set a table and forget it; when guests sit down, check the table setting for changes that can cause you hassles.

3. Give them a *clean* setup.

No diner likes to receive silverware that isn't clean.

When you set the table, check the silverware carefully.

4. Take responsibility for quality control.

Don't bring anything to the table that isn't presentable. Examine everything from the kitchen for cleanliness, correctness, and visual appeal. If an item doesn't make it because of quality or appearance, have it replaced or corrected.

Wipe gravy (or whatever) from the rim of a plate before serving.

5. Practice "safety first".

When repouring coffee or water, pick up the glass or cup and step back so that any spills will miss the customer and the table.

Don't run, especially when you're in a hurry. Running servers eventually fall, drop food or drink, or collide with staff or customers. And, they always look like rookies who are having a tough time handling the job.

Warn customers about very hot dishes.

Use a side towel to pick up and serve hot dishes, to hold a hot or slippery tray, to wipe up a spill at the table, and to wipe the bottom of a plate or tray.

(Side towels, by the way, should be changed often. *As soon as your side towel gets dirty, get a clean one.*)

How to Prevent Complaints of *Unprofessional* Service

1. Keep serving trays off the table.

And keep *yourself* off the table: never lean on the table or a guest's chair.

The same goes for water pitchers, coffee pots, and other tools of your trade. Set them down only on a side stand or other work area.

When you're serving from a tray, keep it away from the table and guests. If it gets dumped, it's easier on everyone if it lands on the floor rather than on the table or on customers' heads.

2. If you sense a problem, investigate.

If food is not being eaten, politely inquire about it. Don't ask, "Is there a problem here?" Make your inquiry specific to the food or service: *Is the steak just the way you wanted it?*

If your guest is dissatisfied, offer to correct or replace the order, or otherwise solve whatever the problem. Communicate your openness to making the food and service outstanding.

3. Keep guests informed.

If an order will be delayed, tell guests right away. There isn't much you can do about a backlog in the kitchen, and your guests will have to wait it out. But it's easier for them to wait if they know the reason for the delay.

Don't let them get the idea that their order is ready—but you've neglected to pick it up.

4. Handle dishes, silverware, glasses properly.

These basic rules of common courtesy are broken surprisingly often:

• Plates should be held on the palm of your hand with your thumb at the rim; no thumbs on top of the plate.

• Cups should be carried on a saucer, or held by the handle, never the rim.

• Glassware should be handled only by the base or stem.

• Silverware should be handled only by the *handle* and with two fingers only.

5. Never serve anything with wet hands.

6. Follow a suitable serving sequence.

The general rule: Children first (girls, then boys); then ladies, then gentlemen.

However, when you have to reach over one diner to serve another (as in a large booth), first serve the person who is *hardest-to-reach*. That way you avoid leaning over someone's food, dragging your apron strings through their soup.

7. Serve from the most convenient side.

The old rules of serving food from the left, beverages from the right are no longer closely followed except in formal dining situations.

When you pick up coffee cups to refill them, put them back *in the same place*. Left-handed coffee drinkers shouldn't have to drag their cup back over to the left side every time they get a refill.

8. Show your labels.

When you serve bottles (ketchup, beer) or jars (mustard) that have labels, set them down with the label facing the customer.

9. Clear the table quickly and *quietly* between courses.

Use a cocktail tray to clear more than two items from the table.

10. Break behavior habits that annoy diners.

Don't chew gum on duty. Don't shout, yell, shriek, or scream. Don't hum or sing. Don't sneeze, cough, or blow your nose.

11. Alert guests to potential problems.

Whenever you suspect that guests may be unpleasantly surprised about something—the size (or seasoning) of a certain dish, or the extra preparation time for an order—don't keep it a secret. Tell them what to expect while they still have time to change the order.

12. Know your priorities.

Professional servers use this sequence:

1) Serve the food—getting hot food out of the kitchen is your first priority with few (if any) exceptions.
2) Reset tables.
3) Greet new customers.

13. Bring one course at a time.

But if a couple orders an appetizer for her, and a salad for him, break the rule of *appetizer first, then salad* and bring both at the same time.

How to Take Orders Without Inviting Complaints

1. Concentrate on one order at a time.

Make sure you understand each guest's order before going on to the next one. Make sure each order is complete: How to cook each steak, what kind of potatoes, what kind of dressing?

2. Identify free extras as "complimentary".

Would you like complimentary *anchovies on your pizza?*
Your entree includes *your choice of…*

3. Include the price when you announce a special that is not included on the menu.

4. Write the price of each item as you write the order.

It takes only a few more seconds, and you may be pressed for time later when things get *really* busy. Whenever there's a chance of confusion, repeat each order aloud as you write it.

5. Use a memory system.

The most irritating question in the restaurant business: "Who gets the… ?" Try the *Home Base System* to help you remember who gets what:

1) Choose your home base—the front door, a clock, the cashier's counter.
2) At each table, the guest closest to the home base is in place number one.
3) The remaining places are numbered clockwise from place number one.
4) Write each guest's place number on the check next to each item ordered.

Or, use the *Senior Guest System* (same as the home base method except the oldest member of the party becomes guest number one).

Or, use the *Striking Feature System* (same as the senior guest method except the guy in the orange suit with the green tie is guest number one).

6. Make changes cheerfully.

It can be exasperating sometimes to change diners' orders after you've written them. But if it makes them happy, it's worth it; happy diners tip better than unhappy diners.

7. Pick up menus as each guest orders.

You'll save time and effort (and reduce frivolous order-changing).

Some Trouble Spots

There are three places in the average dining room where delivering the extras will help you the most.

- At noisy tables near kitchen or service areas.

- At windy tables near the front door.

- At conspicuous tables in the center of the room.

These areas are usually considered to be less desirable by diners. Whatever extra service you can offer to compensate will pay off in fewer complaints and better tips.

How to Turn Problems Into Tips

SOMETIMES, NO MATTER how hard you try to prevent them, problems with food or service will occur.

But they don't have to mar your performance. Instead, problems can give you an opportunity for earning better tips than ever—if you solve them quickly and professionally.

The first rule for solving customer service problems: Treat all problems as opportunities. Many top servers say they *welcome* complaints from customers because it gives them a chance to make everything right.

To most restaurant goers, that's a refreshing change from servers who face trouble by looking the other way and hoping for the best.

The customer is also hoping for the best, and is likely to feel more generous after receiving it.

12 Steps Toward Handling a Complaint—Successfully

How should you handle the customer complaints you can't prevent? Here are a dozen guidelines to follow for effective (and *profitable*) problem-solving.

1. Look at a complaint positively.

Looking at a complaint as an indication that something is wrong, or fouled up, or that the complaint itself is unjustified, makes it difficult to solve satisfactorily.

A slight change in attitude will help.

You'll find that complaints are easier to answer if you approach them with a positive attitude: something simply needs fixing or needs to be completed or, that a simple adjustment is necessary.

2. Consider every complaint to be legitimate.

Very few restaurant goers are out to cheat the house.

Most customers are reluctant to complain when things are not going right. So reluctant, in fact, that they *don't* complain; they just go somewhere else to eat next time.

When customers do tell you that something is not right, accept it as an honest complaint.

3. Listen closely to a complaint.

You need to know what the real problem is to solve it effectively. If the nature of the trouble is unclear, try asking a simple question that can be answered by Yes or No.

4. Don't ask for proof.

Don't let your guest feel you are asking him to prove he's got a legitimate gripe. Any sign of distrust, or resistance to offering immediate help, can only make things worse.

5. Apologize for the error.

This is the most important step, the part so many people in customer service ignore or forget.

Indeed, some servers simply refuse to apologize to customers for anything that has gone wrong, particularly when it's not their fault! That's a mistake.

An apology is neither a confession of guilt nor an admission of incompetence. It's merely an sympathetic expression that shows concern for a guest's comfort. It says, "I care."

Make it simple: *I'm sorry.* Elaborate apologies are unnecessary.

Make it sincere. Look directly at your customer, not at the customer's companion, and not through the window at someone out in the parking lot.

Sincere apologies with eye contact win people over quickly, possibly because they are so rare.

6. Avoid assessing blame.

Don't blame the chef, the busboy, the hostess, the dishwasher, the manager, the heavy crowd, or the system. Don't even take the blame yourself.

And above all, don't blame the customer, *especially if it was the customer's fault.* (He probably already knows it!) Placing the blame squarely where it belongs may make you feel better for a brief moment but then the thrill is gone, and you still have to deal with the problem.

A customer who has been put in his place is likely to leave in an angry mood—and with your tip in his pocket.

7. Take the customer's side.

A server who can handle complaints satisfactorily will be perceived by diners as someone who cares, someone who is working for *them*, not the restaurant.

Of course, when you take the customer's side, you're really working equally hard for the restaurant since satisfactory complaint-handling invites return business and leads to solid recommendations by satisfied customers.

8. Say you'll correct the problem.

Not *try* to correct it; *correct* it.

The difference in wording puts guests at ease, lets them know they're in good hands. They're much more likely to accept your solution to the problem if you've made it clear that you *will* solve it, not just try to solve it.

Don't answer a complaint with, "Would you like me to take care of that?" A better response: *Yes, of course, that's not right, let me take care of that for you (let me fix that for you, let me exchange that for you).*

If your guest responds with "No, that's okay", consider the case closed. Don't dwell on a mistake, or a misunderstanding.

Diners are often placated by your obvious concern for their satisfaction; they won't require you to make things perfect.

Sometimes, just *offering* to fix something is enough.

9. Do something about it—quickly.

It's irritating for diners to receive a rare steak when they order it medium. It's worse to face a long wait for that steak to be repaired while companions are enjoying theirs.

To shorten the wait, make complaint-fixing your highest priority.

10. Keep them posted.

A customer whose complaint is being taken care of appreciates a little feedback.

You could take that steak to the kitchen for further cooking, then go back to your station and serve other guests. Or, you could return to the table first to deliver this brief message: *Your steak is on the grill, sir. I'll have it back for you in a few moments.*

That short message says "Your problem is being solved at this moment and I will not relax until everything has been made right."

Say it with a smile. But not a big smile—try instead for an *apologetic* smile, a subtle expression of concern. You'll have a relaxed, appreciative diner who's on your side. (Just what you want.)

11. Deliver the correction.

No more apologies are necessary; just a simple *Thank you* should serve to say several things:

Thanks for bringing this matter to our attention
Thanks for being so reasonable
Thanks for your patience

12. Make a mental note of the problem.

Think of what you might do to avoid having the same thing happen again. What clues can you look for to identify, then solve, the problem in the future before it prompts a complaint?

How To Handle Rude Behavior

One of the brutal truths of customer service is: *Some people refuse to be satisfied.*

What is worse, they often communicate their dissatisfaction through rude remarks or hostile behavior. Some of their more common obnoxious moves:

- Assuming a superior attitude and attempting to humiliate you
- Grabbing your arm or sleeve to get attention
- Making demands instead of requests
- Snapping their fingers for attention

It's as if these boors were sent to your table as a test of your ability to stay cool in any situation.

Everyone who works in customer service occasionally has to deal with these types. But not everyone handles the problem with equal aplomb.

Staying cool, though, takes most of the sting out of this kind of meeting. Here are a few tricks the pros use to stay cool.

1. Adopt the attitude, *The Customer Is Always Right.*

Important: This does not mean the server is always wrong. It doesn't mean the customer is always right, either!

What this famous motto really means is this: If you hope to earn maximum tips with minimum hassles (as well as good recommendations and repeat business), you have got to treat all customers *as if* they are always right.

2. Assume a neutral position.

Consider yourself to be the representative of restaurant management.

Your job is to accept *management's* responsibility when things go wrong, express *management's* regret for the error, then, pledge *management's* renewed effort in eliminating errors.

Consider any displays of anger, or negative comments made by customers, to have been directed toward the restaurant in general, not directed towards you.

Don't take indirect remarks or expressions personally, especially remarks you overhear in conversation; it's easy to misconstrue remarks people make when you're unaware of the context.

3. Let bad behavior be *their* problem.

When people act rude, impolite, discourteous, obnoxious, or antisocial, dismiss it as a hazard of the job: It comes with the territory.

Let their boorishness be *their* problem, not yours.

4. Defuse anger and hostility with courtesy and charm.

There's just no way you can win by reacting in kind to a hostile question or statement. Don't lower yourself to engage in an argument with a customer. Don't let someone push you into losing your temper.

Here's a tactic the pros say works every time: *The uglier they get, the nicer you get.*

5. Don't let frustrations build up.

Pent-up frustration will negatively affect your performance at other tables. Free yourself of frustration in a constructive way. But don't let off steam in public. One theory has it that when things just get to be too much, it's healthy just "let it all out." Maybe so, but not in the dining room.

Getting into an argument or bitter exchange with customers is at least as unhealthy as keeping everything pent up inside.

If things get out of hand, say *Excuse me, I'll be back in a few moments* to leave an uncomfortable situation. Walk away, take a few deep breaths, count to ten and remind yourself that misunderstandings are a part of life.

Or, walk back to the big refrigerator, close the door behind you and scream!

6. When all else fails, call your manager.

When problems just won't go away (that happens sometimes), you need help. That's one of the things your manager is there for.

Managers are paid to control uncontrollable situations.

Don't Get Discouraged

Don't let tough customer relations get you down. Some people are simply impossible to reason with or deal with. You can't please them, you can't satisfy them, you can't relate to them.

So—just do the best you can, then go on with your work.

The bright side is, guests who have problems solved cheerfully and quickly are apt to become your best word-of-mouth advertisers, and most generous customers.

Solving problems from the customer's point of view is a way of distinguishing yourself as someone to can *make things right* when things go wrong. Few people who work in customer service jobs seem able (or willing) to do that.

Those who *are* able and willing, are often rewarded extra—as if they've performed above and beyond the call of duty.

For a pro, it's just part of the job.

11

How to Retrieve the Table

THE GOOD POINTS you make with guests—from your first *Hello,* to serving dessert—can be lost because of mistakes in the final moments you spend with each party.

Here are some tips that will help you end your performance at each table on a high note, and with no loss of points.

The Prime Time

When is the most appropriate time to present the check?

It can vary from one extreme to the other.

The house policy in most coffee shops, for example, is to present the check when you serve the food. In white-tablecloth dining rooms, the common policy is, present it after your guests have asked for it.

Where policies haven't been set up, it's up to you to decide. Here are some suggestions for presenting the check at the most appropriate time.

- ## Bring the check with the food.

  This is your best bet in a house with frequent customer turnover, and informal and minimal service.

- ## Bring the check when asked for it.

  And don't be surprised if you get asked for it moments after you've delivered the entrees. Many fast-track executives like to get the bill paid so they can eat and run. (These busy guys have no time to wait around for the tab!)

  Most diners, though, will ask for the check as you clear the table after the main course, or after the dessert. You ask if there's anything else you can bring them; they answer, "No thanks, we're ready for the check." It's that simple.

  Important: *When a guest asks for the check, bring it right away.* Don't bus dishes, take other orders, deliver other orders, or chat with anyone until you've delivered that check.

  If they're ready to pay, be ready to accept it. That keeps guests who are in a hurry, happy. And improves your table turnover rate at the same time.

- ## Bring the check when your guests have finished.

  On a busy night, don't wait to be asked; present the check as soon as you're sure your party has finished eating. You can try to determine this by asking, *May I bring you coffee? Or dessert? Anything else then?*

  "No, thanks."

  Smile. Bring the check.

  Note: Keep yourself visible to diners who are finishing their meal. Get the check delivered before guests have their coats on and are on their way to the cashier.

Presenting: The Check!

1. Bring the right check to the right table.

Your party at Table 5 pays the tab you gave them, even though it's only half the amount it should be.

Later, your party at Table 7 points out that the check you've just presented (which should have gone to table 5) is twice the amount it should be.

Don't count on Table 7 to make up the difference.

2. Check your addition.

Writing the check clearly and neatly will help you avoid errors when adding it all up. Use a calculator when you have several figures to add.

Then, double-check your addition.

It's easier to be right—and know you are right—than it is to correct a mistake. (If there is a mistake, you can bet your guests will find it.)

Wait until your guests have finished ordering before totaling the check. Scratch-outs and several subtotals create confusion; the check becomes less readable and errors are more likely to occur.

Write "Thank You!" and sign your name on the check.

3. Present the check—face down—on a tip tray.

Or, use a salad plate; it adds a little class.

4. Set the check near the host.

If it's not obvious who the host is, put it in a convenient place near the center of the table.

To the entire party, a few simple words are appropriate: *Thank you! I hope you all enjoyed your dinner.*

Then to the host, one of the following is a courtesy:

- *You may pay the cashier in front—whenever you're ready.*

- *I'll come back for this—whenever you're ready. We accept Visa, Mastercharge, American Express, cash, or your personal check with I.D.*

- *The maitre d' will pick this up—whenever you're ready.*

5. Always say *Thank You* after presenting the check.

6. Don't walk away if the host is ready to pay.

Look for a sign that your party is ready to pay the tab. An obvious clue: your guest digs into a purse, or reaches for a wallet.

Whenever a customer sets down money for the tab before you've had a chance to bring it, offer the check anyway, face up showing the total before picking up the payment.

7. In case of a problem with the check, stay cool.

Example: If a guest accuses you of presenting an incorrect check, your first reaction should be *neutral*. Don't look offended, don't look incredulous, don't look embarrassed. Just say, *I'm sorry, we can correct that. Where is the error?*

If it turns out your guest has erred, simply explain the error as clearly as you can by stating facts. Avoid including your guest in the explanation with phrases like, *"You* probably thought...; Here's where *you're* mistaken...; *You* forgot to include..."

Your objective is merely to clear up the confusion, not to show who's right and who's wrong.

If it's you who have erred, simply say *You're absolutely right. The mistake is mine. I'm sorry. I'll correct this right away.*

When you re-submit your corrected tab, don't apologize again or refer to the mistake again, just say *Thank you.* (You can't say that too often.)

How to Handle the Request for Separate Checks

For parties of two, give separate checks *whenever asked*. For parties of three or more, give separate checks cheerfully *when it's simple and convenient for you.*

If, instead, you're busy with other tables and your party's order is complicated, try this: Suggest separate *receipts*.

Returning the Change

1. Return *all* change to the table.

Customers may put enough money on the tip tray to cover the tab, plus the tip. Return *all* of the change. Never assume the change is meant as a tip.

2. Make convenient change.

Make it easy for your guest to leave a maximum tip. For example, if the change is:

- $ 5, return 5 ones
- $10, return 1 five and 5 ones
- $15, return 2 fives and 5 ones
- $20, return 1 ten, 1 five, and five ones

Note: *If house policy forbids breaking change this way, carry enough change to break it for the customer who requests it at the table.*

3. Always say *Thank you* after returning the change.

4. Don't concern yourself with the tip.

Resist the urge to scoop up the tip too early. Leave tips on the table while customers are still seated (unless a tip is passed over to you).

If the tip on the table is not as generous as you'd like it to be, your disappointment can affect your performance in the closing minutes.

The pros say the more you think about tips, the greater your chances of disappointment. The more you think about customer service, the more likely you are to receive tips.

Personal Checks

If your restaurant accepts checks, the following steps may help you weed out some of the bad ones:

1. Check the date.
Never accept a check with no date, an old date, or a check dated in advance.

2. Check the bank's location.
The check should show the name, branch, town, and state where the bank is located. If it's an out-of-state bank, your house policy may rule out your accepting it.

3. Check the amount.
Be sure the written amount is the same as the numerical amount.

4. Check it for legibility.
Don't accept a check that's unreadable. It should be signed in ink. It should have no erasures, and no written-over amounts.

5. Check the payee.
It should be made out to *your restaurant.*

6. Know your house policy on accepting government checks.
Some banks refuse to cash social security, welfare, relief, or income tax checks for third parties. In this type of transaction, your restaurant is a third party.

7. Watch for forged checks.

Some forged check facts:

• Most are passed in October, November, and December.

• Most have low check numbers (1 to 150) in the upper right hand corner.

• More than half the forged checks are passed with *expired* drivers' licenses. Check the expiration date on the license, write it on the front of the check, and initial it.

Credit Cards

If your restaurant accepts credit cards, here are some tips to help you process them quickly and smoothly:

1. Look at the card.

Is it valid? Check the date. Is it signed? Check the reverse side.

2. Be careful running a card through the machine.

Make sure the receipt gets printed clearly.

3. Check the name on the front.

Is it a man's or woman's name? When returning with a credit slip for signature, make sure you give it to the right person!

4. Record your tips.

Before you submit your credit slips to the cashier, make a note of your tips that are to be paid later (once a week is common).

How to Get Your Table Back

Your guests have finished eating. They have paid the check. But they're still sitting there talking, and you need the table.

This is going to require some tactful diplomacy if you want to avoid annoying satisfied customers.

You might start by returning to the table and asking once again, *Is there anything else?* Most people will get the hint. But if they answer, "No thanks, we're fine here", you've got your work cut out for you.

Try the I'm-in-trouble, can-you-help? ploy: *I'm sorry, I hate to ask this, but I'm really on the spot. We have several people who have been waiting for a table and I don't have any place to seat them. I was hoping you might not mind?*

Another tactic which often works: *May we offer you a complimentary drink in the bar?*

Watch Out for Check-beaters

Some customers overstay their welcome.

Others *understay* theirs: they don't even stay long enough to pay the check.

You may occasionally have this problem with kids. They're tough to control, especially in a group. If you suspect they may be planning to beat the check, pass the word to the manager, host, and other servers to help you keep an eye on them.

Often, if you give them the feeling you're on to their plan, they'll decide against it.

But all check-beaters are not thrill-seeking teenagers:

A well-dressed couple took a corner table for four. They set their department store shopping bags (full of Christmas packages) on the other two chairs. They ate an expensive meal. Then, as they ordered after-dinner drinks, the lady asked for directions to the powder room; her companion asked for directions to the telephone. They never returned for the drinks. Or the check. Or to pick up their Christmas shopping bags. The bags had been filled with crumpled newspaper and topped off with empty gift-wrapped boxes.

It was an elaborate hoax, but the check-beaters enjoyed an expensive lunch for their trouble. The house lost the tab, the server lost the tip.

Fortunately, losses from schemes like that are relatively rare. But it's good to be aware of the trouble some people will go to in order to beat you.

Try to keep on top of it.

Savvy Sayonaras

Your job's not over until you've personally thanked everyone, invited them back, and said good bye. Intercept your guests when they leave. Try not to let anybody you've served get out the door without a final thank you and a smile.

Check the table for coats, hats, wallets, or other forgotten items; get them returned before your guests get out the door.

Then, *pick up the tip.*

It should be the *maximum* tip, because your performance was first-rate:

Your *service* was attentive and intelligent, polished, polite, watchful, available, prompt, efficient, clairvoyant, thoughtful, devoted, sophisticated, egalitarian, friendly, and helpful.

And *you* were gracious and attractive, adaptable, versatile, diplomatic, tactful, cheerful, courteous, sensitive, considerate, and poised.

Congratulations!

Next, how to keep your share of the tips you've earned.

12

How to Keep Your Share

ANOTHER DAY, ANOTHER $100. Too bad you can't keep it all. Some of it goes to the buser, some to the bartender, some to the taxman.

Contrary to popular belief, however, it *is* possible to give everyone else their fair share and still have a fair share for yourself, even after taxes.

The tax laws on reporting income from tips are widely misunderstood. Some servers may be paying more taxes than required; others are certainly paying less than required.

The first group can probably find better things to do with tips than to split them freely with Uncle Sam.

The second group risks paying heavy penalties, in addition to back taxes, if their returns are audited.

In this chapter are some tax rules you need to know to keep your taxes legally low and avoid paying penalties.

(For the full story of taxes on tips, get a copy of Internal Revenue Service Publication 531, *Reporting Income From Tips,* and Publication 17, *Your Federal Income Tax,* from your nearest IRS office, or by mail.)

Questions, and Answers From IRS Publications 531 & 17

What percentage of my tips are taxable?

All tips you receive are subject to federal income tax. You must include in gross income tips you receive directly from customers, tips from charge customers that are paid to you by your employer, and your share of any tips you receive under a tip-splitting arrangement.

In addition, cash tips of $20 or more that you receive in a month while working for any one employer are subject to withholding of income tax and social security or railroad retirement tax.

What percentage of my tips do I have to report to my employer?

If you receive less than $20 in tips while working for one employer during one month, you do not have to report them to that employer. But you must include the tips in gross income on your income tax return. There is no social security or railroad retirement tax on these tips.

If you receive tips of $20 or more in a month while working for any one employer, you must report the total amount of your tips to that employer by the 10th day of the next month.

Tip splitting. If you split tips with fellow employees, such as waiters giving a part of their tips to busboys, you include only your share of the tips in your report to your employer.

Service charges. A club, hotel, or restaurant may require customers who use its dining or banquet rooms to pay a service charge, which is given to the waiters and waitresses and other employees. Your share of this service charge is not a tip, but is part of your wages paid by the employer. You should not include your share in your report of tips to your employer. Your employer should not include it in tips paid to you, but should include it in your wages.

What kind of records do I have to keep?

You should keep a daily record of your tips. This will help you prepare any written report you are required to give your employer. If you receive or pay out tips under a tip-splitting arrangement, it will also be helpful to you to keep a record of these tips for preparing your income tax return.

You must be able to substantiate the amount of tip income you receive during the year. Beginning in October 1985, there are new rules about the records you must keep to establish your tip income.

New recordkeeping rules. For tips you receive after September 1985, you must keep a **daily record** or **other evidence** to substantiate the amount of tip income you report on your return.

Daily record. Your daily record must show your name and address, your employer's name, and, if different, the establishment's name. It must also show, for each workday, the amount of cash and charge tips you received directly from customers or from other employees, the amount of tips you paid out to other employees, and the names of the other employees to whom you paid out tips.

You must make the entries in your daily record on or near the date you receive the tip income.

You can use Form 4070-A, *Employee's Daily Record of Tips,* to keep this record.

Other evidence. If you do not keep a daily record of tips, you must maintain other evidence of the tip income you receive. This other evidence must be as credible and reliable as a daily record. This other evidence can be documentary evidence that shows tips added to a check and paid over to you or amounts paid for food or beverages with respect to which you would generally receive a tip. Examples of documentary evidence are copies of restaurant bills and credit card charges that contain amounts added by customers as tips.

How can I stop taxes from being withheld from my paycheck?

Your employer must withhold social security or railroad retirement tax and any income taxes due on tips you report. Your employer usually deducts the withholding due on tips from your regular wages. But you do not have to have income taxes withheld if you had no tax liability last year and expect none this year.

Income tax will not be taken out of your pay if you give your employer a filled in Form W-4, Employee's Withholding Allowance Certificate, claiming an exemption from withholding.

Form 4070-A (Rev. August 1985) — Employee's Daily Record of Tips — OMB No. 1545-0065

Employee's name and address: John W. Allen, 1117 Maple Ave., Anytown, NY 14202
Employer's name: Parkview Restaurant
Establishment's name (if different):
Month and year: January 1986

Date	a. Tips received directly from customers and other employees	b. Tips received on charge receipts	c. Tips paid out to other employees	d. Names of employees to whom tips were paid out
1	Closed	—	—	
2	48.80	26.40	8.80	Judy Brown, Brian Smith
3	28.00	21.60	9.60	Judy Brown, Carl Jones
4	42.00	24.00	10.00	Judy Brown, Carl Jones
5	40.80	28.00	12.00	Judy Brown, Carl Jones
Subtotals	159.60	100.00	45.20	

Date	a.	b.	c.	d.
6	off			
7	37.20	22.40	8.00	Carl Jones, Brian Smith
8	50.80	17.20	10.00	Judy Brown, Carl Jones
9	33.60	16.40	8.00	Judy Brown, Brian Smith
10	20.40	22.00	9.20	Judy Brown, Carl Jones
11	42.00	11.60	8.80	Judy Brown, Carl Jones
12	38.60	16.00	8.80	Judy Brown, Carl Jones
13	off			
14	48.40	14.40	12.40	Carl Jones, Brian Smith
15	46.20	32.00	17.20	Judy Brown, Carl Jones
Subtotals	327.20	152.00	81.20	

Date	a.	b.	c.	d.
16	41.20	18.40	8.80	Judy Brown, Brian Smith
17	39.20	21.20	9.60	Judy Brown, Carl Jones
18	46.80	12.80	8.40	Judy Brown, Carl Jones
19	34.00	19.20	10.00	Judy Brown, Carl Jones
20	off			
21	34.80	26.00	12.80	Carl Jones, Brian Smith
22	42.40	22.80	12.40	Judy Brown, Carl Jones
23	48.80	17.20	13.60	Judy Brown, Brian Smith
24	33.60	19.20	10.80	Judy Brown, Carl Jones
25	37.20	14.80	9.20	Judy Brown, Carl Jones
Subtotals	359.00	171.60	95.60	

Date	a.	b.	c.	d.
26	31.60	11.60	12.40	Judy Brown, Carl Jones
27	off			
28	43.20	14.00	12.80	Carl Jones, Brian Smith
29	34.90	22.40	7.20	Judy Brown, Carl Jones
30	46.00	27.20	12.90	Judy Brown, Carl Jones
31	22.60	20.40	6.40	Judy Brown, Carl Jones
Subtotals from pages 1, 2 and 3	137.60 / 123.20 / 159.00	109.00 / 152.00 / 171.60	45.20 / 81.20 / 95.60	
Totals	1024.00	519.20	223.60	

Tips (col. a plus col. b minus col. c). Report this amount on Form 4070 ▶ 1269.60

Form 4070 (Rev. August 1985) — Department of the Treasury, Internal Revenue Service
Employee's Report of Tips to Employer
▶ For Paperwork Reduction Act Notice, see back of this form.
OMB No. 1545-0065

Employee's name and address: John W. Allen, 1117 Maple Ave., Anytown, NY 14202
Social security number: 987 00 4321
Employer's name and address: Parkview Restaurant, 834 Main Ave., Anytown, NY 14203

Month or shorter period in which tips were received
from January 1, 1986 to January 31, 1986
Tips: $1,269.60
Signature: John W. Allen
Date: February 3, 1986

Forms 4070-A & 4070 from IRS Publication 1244

To order additional copies of Maximum Tips, use this coupon

YES! Please send me:

_____ copies of Maximum Tips @ $12.95 each

Name: _____

Address: _____

City: _____ State: ___ Zip: _____

Shipping/handling: $1.50 for the first book, 50 cents for each additional book.

If you live in California, please add 78 cents for CA sales tax.

Send order to:

SFO Press
55 New Montgomery Street
San Francisco, CA 94105